Canadian Supplement for Industrial Organization

Second Edition

Andrew Eckert
University of Alberta

Douglas S. West
University of Alberta

PEARSON

Addison
Wesley

Toronto

ISBN 0-321-30698-8

Senior Acquisitions Editor: Gary Bennett
Developmental Editor: Angela Kurmey
Production Editor: Marisa D'Andrea
Production Coordinator: Andrea Falkenberg

Statistics Canada information is used with the permission of the Minister of Industry, as Minister responsible for Statistics Canada. Information on the availability of the wide range of data from Statistics Canada can be obtained from Statistics Canada's Regional Offices, its World Wide Web site at http://www.statcan.ca, and its toll-free access number 1-800-263-1136.

2 3 4 DPC 07 06 05

Printed and bound in Canada.

PEARSON
Addison
Wesley

To Alice and Heather
                        —A.E.

To Jessica, Niki, and Kathy
                        —D.S.W.

TABLE OF CONTENTS

PREFACE

Canadian Supplement for Industrial Organization, Second Edition, has been written to provide Canadian users of Dennis Carlton and Jeffrey Perloff's text, *Modern Industrial Organization*, with a broad survey of Canadian market structure, firm behaviour, and economic regulations (including Canadian competition policy) affecting business enterprises in Canada. However, *Canadian Supplement for Industrial Organization* can also be used in conjunction with any other industrial organization text.

The five chapters in this book have been written to supplement chapters typically found in industrial organization texts. Chapter 1 contains an overview of the Canadian economy and reviews recent evidence on Canadian corporate size, foreign ownership, crown corporations, privatization, and international trade.

Chapter 2 contains a survey of recent studies of Canadian market structure, merger activity, scale economies, entry/exit activity, and industrial performance. It can be used with Chapters 2, 3, and 8 of Carlton and Perloff's text.

Chapter 3 provides a brief discussion of Canadian patent activity, research and development, and patent policy as applied to the pharmaceutical industry in Canada, and can supplement Carlton and Perloff's Chapter 16.

Chapter 4 contains a discussion of competition policy in Canada and examines various provisions of the *Competition Act*, the Competition Bureau's enforcement policy, and recent decisions of the Competition Tribunal. This chapter can supplement Carlton and Perloff's Chapter 19.

Finally, Chapter 5 contains a discussion of regulation and deregulation of several important industries in Canada, specifically telecommunications and transportation industries, including rail, truck, and air transport. This chapter can be assigned in conjunction with Carlton and Perloff's Chapter 20.

ACKNOWLEDGMENTS

We would like to thank the editorial staff at Pearson Education Canada, and particularly Gary Bennett and Angela Kurmey, for helping see this project through to completion. We would also like to thank Matt Smith and Mary O'Connell for their helpful research assistance, and Charlene Hill for her excellent word processing services.

CHAPTER 1

THE CANADIAN ECONOMY

I. INTRODUCTION

To understand Canadian industrial organization and how it differs from industrial organization in the U.S., it is helpful to have a general description of the economic context within which firms in Canada operate and compete. This chapter is concerned with that context. It begins in the next section with a description of the breakdown of gross domestic product (GDP) and manufacturing industries in Canada and of GDP by industry sector. This is followed in Section III by a discussion of Canadian corporate size, and how Canadian corporations compare with corporations in the rest of the world.

Section IV presents a description of aggregate concentration in Canadian industry. Section V examines the extent of foreign ownership of Canadian industry. Section VI considers the importance of Crown corporations in Canada, and the move in the past two decades towards privatization of public enterprises. Section VII discusses the significance of international trade in Canada, the role of the tariff, and the impacts of free trade. A summary concludes the chapter.

II. THE INDUSTRIAL COMPOSITION OF THE CANADIAN ECONOMY

Table 1.1 shows a breakdown of GDP by industry sector for the years 1981, 1991, and 2001. For agriculture, forestry, fishing, and hunting, there has been a decline in share of GDP from 1981 to 2001 (continuing a trend evident from at least 1961). There is also a noticeable decline in the share of Canadian GDP accounted for by construction, accommodation and food industries, health and social industries, education, and public administration. Certain sectors have picked up significant shares of GDP between 1981 and 2001, particularly trade, the finance, insurance, and real estate industries, professional and related industries, and information and cultural industries.

Table 1.2 reports, for each manufacturing industry in Canada in 1999, the number of establishments, number of employees, value added, and value added as a percent of the total manufacturing value added. The largest group of manufacturing industries measured by value added and total employees is transportation equipment, and the food

Table 1.1
Composition of GDP by Industry Sector[a] ($000,000)

Industry Sector	1981	Percent	1991	Percent	2001	Percent
Agriculture, forestry, fishing, and hunting	17,716	3.17	20,636	2.96	21,316	2.27
Mining	21,555	3.85	28,088	4.03	36,703	3.90
Utilities	18,834	3.37	23,578	3.38	27,568	2.93
Manufacturing	95,494	17.08	109,282	15.67	162,713	17.31
Construction	41,451	7.41	4,350	6.36	50,238	5.35
Transportation	25,367	4.54	31,184	4.47	43,394	4.62
Trade	52,351	9.36	70,407	10.10	107,465	11.43
Finance, insurance, and real estate	98,098	17.54	131,522	18.86	183,902	19.57
Administrative & support	9,163	1.64	15,384	2.21	20,354	2.17
Professional & related	13,870	2.48	20,682	2.97	40,508	4.31
Recreation	5,900	1.06	6,225	0.89	8,769	0.93
Information & cultural	13,894	2.48	21,905	3.14	43,770	4.66
Accommodation & food	18,663	3.34	17,253	2.47	22,505	2.39
Health & social	37,845	6.77	50,871	7.29	53,628	5.71
Educational	37,052	6.63	42,153	6.04	43,317	4.61
Public administration	40,190	7.19	49,375	7.08	52,873	5.63
Other services	11,792	2.11	14,539	2.08	20,878	2.22
TOTAL	**559,235**		**697,434**		**939,901**	

[a]GDP was calculated at factor cost in 1997 prices.

Source: Adapted from the Statistics Canada publication *Canadian Economic Observer*, Historical Statistical Supplement, 2001/2002, Catalogue 11-210, Vol. 16, Table 4, July 2002, pp. 21–22.

industries group follows this. The third and fourth largest industry groups in terms of value added are the computer and electronic product group and the chemical product group, respectively, but these are only eleventh and thirteenth largest when measured by the number of employees. Clearly the ranking of industry size depends upon whether size is measured by employment or value added, and presumably would also depend upon whether size is measured by assets or sales.

Table 1.2
Manufacturing Industries of Canada, 1999

	Establish-ments	Total Employees	Value Added ($000)	Value Added as Percent of Total Manufacturing Value Added
Total All Manufacturing	**29,822**	**1,487,098**	**202,930,229**	
Food mfg.	3,467	167,818	18,364,225	9.05
Beverage & tobacco product mfg.	227	15,857	7,159,728	3.53
Textile mills	374	21,779	1,854,387	0.92
Textile product mills	422	14,856	1,072,833	0.53
Clothing mfg.	1,342	70,744	3,536,227	1.74
Leather & allied product mfg.	176	9,040	432,066	0.21
Wood product mfg.	2,144	115,756	12,280,293	6.05
Paper mfg.	663	82,254	13,782,482	6.79
Printing/related support activities	2,623	59,849	5,298,584	2.61
Petroleum & coal products mfg.	204	6,691	2,384,650	1.18
Chemical mfg.	1,274	55,052	14,331,092	7.06
Plastics & rubber products mfg.	1,436	96,126	9,010,803	4.44
Non-metallic mineral product mfg.	1,354	36,462	4,864,745	2.40
Primary metal mfg.	478	75,594	13,261,554	6.54
Fabricated metal product mfg.	4,283	140,721	11,842,183	5.84
Machinery mfg.	2,653	105,705	11,908,465	5.87
Computer & electronic product mfg.	956	63,812	14,465,347	7.13
Electric equipment/appliance/component	605	39,509	4,221,218	2.08
Transportation equipment mfg.	1,332	195,255	44,659,585	22.01
Furniture & related product mfg.	1,748	72,957	5,196,278	2.56
Miscellaneous mfg.	2,061	41,261	2,998,484	1.48

Source: Adapted from the Statistics Canada publication *Manufacturing Industries of Canada: National and Provincial Areas, 1999*, Catalogue 31-203, Tables 39 and 40, June 2002, pp. 232 and 243.

III. CANADIAN CORPORATE SIZE

Over the years, there have been frequent policy discussions regarding the size and ownership of Canadian firms and their ability to compete in the global economy. While not wishing to address the question of global competition here, it is useful to have some idea of the size of Canadian firms relative to potential global competitors, and the extent of foreign ownership and public ownership of Canadian corporations. Table 1.3 shows the revenues, number of employees, extent of foreign ownership, and major shareholders of the 25 largest corporations in Canada in 2002. Four of the 25 largest companies are subsidiaries of American corporations, while one is a subsidiary of a Japanese corporation. Seven of the 25 largest companies are owned and/or controlled by individual shareholders or families. A provincial government owns only one of the top 25 corporations. A variety of industries is represented in the list of the top 25 companies, including telecommunications, automotive, retail, transportation, banking, petroleum, insurance, and power.

To put the sizes of Canada's largest firms in perspective, Table 1.4 reports the sales and numbers of employees for Canadian and selected non-Canadian corporations among the world's 500 largest corporations in 2002. Only 14 Canadian corporations are on the list of the world's 500 largest corporations. The largest Canadian industrial corporation, George Weston, ranks 269th on the list and has sales that are 7.1 percent of Wal-Mart's sales.

IV. CORPORATE CONCENTRATION

In 1975, the Royal Commission on Corporate Concentration was appointed "to inquire into, report upon, and make recommendations concerning: (a) the nature and role of major concentrations of corporate power in Canada; (b) the economic and social implications for the public interest of such concentrations; and (c) whether safeguards exist or may be required to protect the public interest in the presence of such concentrations."[1] As part of the Royal Commission's inquiry, a variety of studies were commissioned, including corporate background reports, corporate case studies, social implications studies, and technical reports and economic studies of concentration, scale economies and mergers. With respect to the question of industrial concentration in

---

[1] See *Report of the Royal Commission on Corporate Concentration* (1978, p. xix). Reproduced with the permission of the Minister of Public Works and Government Services Canada, 2004, and courtesy of the Privy Council Office.

Table 1.3
Canada's 25 Largest Corporations, 2002

Rank	Corporation	Revenues ($000)	Employees	Percent Foreign Ownership	Major Shareholder(s)
1	General Motors of Canada Ltd.	37,000,000	24,500	100	General Motors, U.S.
2	George Weston Ltd.	27,446,000	139,000		W. Galen Weston, 62%
3	Bombardier Inc.	23,664,900	75,000		Bombardier Family, 63%
4	Ford Motor Co. of Canada	23,328,700	15,074	100	Ford Motor Co., U.S.
5	Royal Bank of Canada	23,234,000	59,549	20	Widely held
6	Sun Life Financial Services of Canada	23,101,000	11,800		Widely held
7	Onex Corp.	22,653,000	98,000		Gerald Schwartz, 67% voting
8	Magna International	20,364,470	73,000		Stronach Trust, 58%
9	BCE Inc.	19,768,000	66,266	14	Widely held
10	Alcan Inc.	19,687,000	50,000		Widely held
11	Daimler Chrysler Canada Inc.	19,353,000	NA	100	Daimler Chrysler Corp., U.S.
12	Power Corp. of Canada	19,017,000	28,000		Paul Desmarais Sr., 65%
13	Bank of Nova Scotia	18,310,000	49,000		Widely held
14	CIBC	17,055,000	42,552		Widely held
15	Imperial Oil Ltd.	16,890,000	6,460	70	Exxon Mobil Corp., U.S.
16	Toronto-Dominion Bank	16,680,000	42,817		Widely held
17	Nortel Networks Corp.	16,538,380	52,600		Widely held
18	Manulife Financial Corp.	16,532,000	32,400		Widely held
19	Bank of Montreal	13,059,000	33,000		Widely held
20	Hydro-Quebec	13,002,000	20,972		Quebec government
21	Honda Canada Inc.	12,300,000	4,600	100	Honda Motor Co. Ltd., Japan
22	Thompson Corp.	12,176,920	44,000		Woodbridge C., 69%
23	Quebecor Inc.	12,014,000	50,000		Placements Peladeau, 64%
24	En Cana Corp.	10,011,000	3,646	48	Widely held
25	Empire Co. Ltd.	9,926,500	34,000		Sobey Family, 72%

Source: "FP500 Canada's 500 Largest Corporations," *National Post Business*, Don Mills: National Post., June 2003, p. 68.

Table 1.4
Canadian and Selected Non-Canadian Corporations among the World's 500 Largest Corporations, 2002

World Rank	Corporations	Country	Revenues (U.S. $000,000)
1	Wal-Mart Stores	U.S.	246,525.0
50	Merck	U.S.	51,790.3
100	Sumitomo Life Insurance	Japan	36,304.5
150	Valero Energy	U.S.	26,976.3
200	Electronic Data Systems	U.S.	21,782.0
250	Visteon	U.S.	18,395.0
269	George Weston	Canada	17,476.0
300	Northwestern Mutual	U.S.	15,916.4
323	Sun Life Financial Services	Canada	15,311.1
329	Bombardier	Canada	15,115.9
337	Royal Bank of Canada	Canada	14,771.7
344	Onex	Canada	14,424.1
350	Swiss Life Insurance & Pension	Switzerland	14,124.5
390	BCE	Canada	13,020.7
391	Magna International	Canada	12,971.0
400	Halliburton	U.S.	12,572.0
402	Alcan	Canada	12,540.0
418	Power Corp. of Canada	Canada	12,108.9
432	Bank of Nova Scotia	Canada	11,663.1
450	Fuji Heavy Industries	Japan	11,262.5
464	CIBC	Canada	10,835.8
470	Nortel Networks	Canada	10,701.0
476	Toronto-Dominion Bank	Canada	10,597.5
479	Manulife Financial	Canada	10,526.6
500	Kawasaki Heavy Industries	Japan	10,173.1

Source: "The Global 500: The World's Largest Corporations," *Fortune*, N.Y.: Time Inc., July 21, 2003, pp. 106–112. FORTUNE, Global 500 © 2003 Time Inc. All rights reserved.

Note: Revenue figures for non-U.S. companies have been converted to U.S. dollars at the average exchange rate during each company's fiscal year. Rankings in this table can differ from the rankings in Table 1.3 because of different average exchange rates being used to convert Canadian dollars.

Canada, the Royal Commission summarized its findings as follows:[2]

1. Aggregate concentration (i.e., the percentage of economic activity accounted for by the largest firms in Canada) decreased from 1923 to 1975; however, the greatest portion of this decrease took place before 1966. Since 1966, aggregate concentration in Canada has changed very little.
2. The average size of Canada's 100 largest non-financial corporations and the average size of Canada's 25 largest financial corporations are very much smaller than the average size of their counterparts in the United States and other developed countries.
3. Aggregate concentration is higher in Canada than in the United States.
4. Industrial concentration … increased in Canadian manufacturing industries from 1948 to 1972. Most of the increase took place between 1948 and 1954. Industrial concentration has remained quite stable from 1965 to 1972.
5. Industrial concentration in Canada is substantially higher than in comparable industries in the United States.

Thus the Commission found that Canadian firms tended to be small relative to large firms in the rest of the world, but large relative to the size of Canadian industries. The Commission then suggested that policymakers face the possible problem of promoting larger Canadian firms, which could increase industrial concentration and lead to adverse competitive effects. Promoting larger Canadian firms so that scale economies could be realised is arguably one of the principal motivations of the North American Free Trade Agreement (see Section VII).

The Commission appeared to be concerned with the same tradeoff that Williamson (1968) focused on in his analysis of merger: the tradeoff between the market power effects of horizontal mergers that increase concentration and possible efficiency gains from the exploitation of scale economies. The topic of merger will be taken up in Chapters 2 and 4, and scale economies and concentration by industry will be addressed in Chapter 2.

---

[2] See *Report of the Royal Commission on Corporate Concentration* (1978, pp. 11–12). Reproduced with the permission of the Minister of Public Works and Government Services Canada, 2004, and courtesy of the Privy Council Office.

The concern over aggregate concentration and corporate concentration has subsided in Canada. There are no recent academic studies on the topic, and the latest available data on aggregate concentration is for 1988.[3] One possible explanation for this seeming indifference to the topic is the recognition that concentration is more usefully measured at the level of individual markets. If an individual market is highly concentrated, firms might exercise market power by charging supra-competitive prices. Since an industry or combination of industries may contain a large number of separate markets, aggregate statistics are not particularly useful in predicting whether market power is being exercised.

V. FOREIGN OWNERSHIP

The extent of foreign ownership of the Canadian economy has been a long-standing concern of many Canadians. McFetridge (1986) characterized the foreign ownership debate as being between "nationalists," who argue that foreign ownership reduces both static efficiency and the potential rate of growth, and "continentalists," who argue the reverse. The nationalists are said to believe that the inefficiency resulting from foreign ownership is due to a "miniature replica effect" (i.e., using plants that are too small to be efficient) and the slow growth is due to an inability to develop and exploit new technologies. The continentalists are said to believe that the multinational enterprise is a vehicle for the transmission of new technologies to Canada (even if foreign firms do spend less on research and development in Canada than Canadian firms).

To help appreciate why foreign ownership has been such a contentious issue, it will be useful to have a description of the extent of foreign ownership of Canadian industry. Table 1.5 shows the total assets and revenues of foreign-controlled and Canadian-controlled corporations for 1990, 1995, and 2000. Foreign-controlled assets accounted for almost 21 percent of total assets in 1990, but fell to a little over 20 percent by 2000. Foreign-controlled revenues, on the other hand, accounted for around 25.5 percent of total revenues in 1990, and increased to just over 30 percent by 2000. Over the decade of the 1990s, Statistics Canada reports that the assets of foreign-controlled corporations grew at virtually the same rate as Canadian-controlled corporations: a 77 percent increase

---

[3] See Statistics Canada (1991).

Table 1.5
Total Corporate Assets and Revenue by Foreign and Canadian Control, 1990, 1995, and 2000

Assets ($000,000)

	Foreign					Canadian			
Year[a]	U.S.	E.U.	Other	Total	Percent of Foreign and Canadian	Private Enterprise	Public Enterprise	Total	Percent of Foreign and Canadian
1990	228,918	142,493	81,188	452,599	20.95	1,457,626	249,930	1,707,556	79.05
1995	313,635	176,747	76,491	566,873	21.45	1,806,713	269,306	2,076,020	78.55
2000	471,532	248,099	90,153	809,785	20.34	2,851,096	321,009	3,172,104	79.66

Revenues ($000,000)

	Foreign					Canadian			
Year[a]	U.S.	E.U.	Other	Total	Percent of Foreign and Canadian	Private Enterprise	Public Enterprise	Total	Percent of Foreign and Canadian
1990	206,671	71,705	44,776	323,152	25.43	876,809	71,026	947,835	74.57
1995	305,180	79,591	62,839	447,614	30.13	968,470	69,680	1,038,151	69.87
2000	458,668	159,537	85,224	703,427	30.38	1,527,410	84,669	1,612,078	69.62

[a]Figures for 1990 and 1995 are the totals for all industries (excluding investment and holding companies); figures for 2000 are the totals for all industries (excluding management of companies and enterprises).

Source: Adapted from the Statistics Canada publication *Corporations Returns Act*, Catalogue 61-220, 1998 (Appendix Table 19) and 2000 (Appendix Table 25).

versus an 81 percent increase.[4] During the 1990s, foreign-controlled revenue more than doubled, while Canadian-controlled revenue rose by around 79 percent.

With respect to the geographic source of foreign control, the United States accounted for just over 50 percent of foreign-controlled Canadian assets and 64 percent of foreign-

[4] See Statistics Canada (2003, p. 8).

controlled Canadian revenue in 1990. These numbers increased to 58 percent and 65 percent, respectively, in 2000. The European Union accounted for around 31 percent of foreign-controlled Canadian assets and 22 percent of foreign-controlled Canadian revenues in 1990, and these numbers were approximately the same in 2000.

Table 1.5 also contains an interesting breakdown of Canadian assets and revenue by private and public enterprise. It shows that private enterprise has increased its share of Canadian-controlled corporate assets from around 85 to 90 percent between 1990 and 2000, while private enterprise increased its share of Canadian-controlled corporate revenue from around 92.5 percent to almost 95 percent. As we will see shortly, these numbers are consistent with the increasing privatization of Canadian industry over the past 10 to 20 years.

Large foreign-controlled companies control relatively small fractions of Canadian assets and revenues. For 1998, Statistics Canada reports that the Canadian-controlled enterprises (all industries) in the list of the 25 largest global enterprises accounted for 36.3 percent of Canadian assets in 1998, while foreign-controlled enterprises in the top 25 controlled only 4.9 percent of Canadian assets. With respect to revenue, the Canadian-controlled enterprises in the top 25 accounted for 8 percent of Canadian revenue in 1998, while foreign-controlled companies controlled 5.4 percent of Canadian revenue.[5]

Foreign control of Canadian assets is not spread uniformly across industries. Rather, as Table 1.6 shows, certain industries, such as manufacturing, oil and gas extraction and coal mining, and wholesale trade, tend to have a greater concentration of foreign control. Table 1.6 reports the dollar value of foreign- and Canadian-controlled Canadian assets by non-financial industry for 2000. The percentage of foreign ownership by industry appears in the last column. One industry that one might expect to have a high degree of foreign control is retailing. Certainly, some large U.S.-based retail chains (e.g., Wal-Mart, Home Depot, Blockbuster, Toys 'R' Us, to name a few) have opened hundreds of stores in Canada. However, only 18 percent of retail assets are under foreign control. Some industries, like segments of the transportation, telecommunications, and banking industries, are subject to government regulations that restrict the degree of foreign control.

---

[5] See Statistics Canada (2001, p. 38).

Table 1.6
Assets by Country of Control by Industry, 2000
Non-financial sector

Industry	Foreign	Canadian ($000,000)	All	Foreign Percent
Manufacturing	266,390	323,091	589,481	45
Real estate and rental and leasing companies	28,692	155,398	184,090	16
Utilities	5,578	173,192	178,770	3
Wholesale trade	60,608	99,726	160,334	38
Oil and gas extraction and coal mining	67,102	90,941	158,043	42
Information and culture	6,585	148,531	155,116	4
Transportation and warehousing	17,253	100,452	117,705	15
Retail trade	20,127	90,558	110,685	18
Construction	4,204	86,667	90,871	5
Mining (except oil, gas, and coal)	20,218	62,621	82,839	24
Professional, scientific, and technical services	13,241	59,612	72,853	18
Agriculture, forestry, fishing, and hunting	1,065	44,841	45,906	2
Accommodation and food services	4,988	29,104	34,092	15
Administrative and support, waste management, and remediation services	8,419	23,096	31,515	27
Other services (except public administration)	*	22,654	26,051	*
Health care and social assistance	*	17,686	18,253	*
Arts, entertainment, and recreation	729	14,589	15,318	5
Educational services	141	2,340	2,481	6
Total non-financial industries	529,301	1,545,097	2,074,398	26

*Too unreliable to be published by Statistics Canada.

Source: Adapted from the Statistics Canada (2003) publication *Corporations Returns Act*, Catalogue 61-220, 2000, p. 17.

Globerman (1999) has summarized some of the arguments that have been made for restrictions on ownership of certain Canadian industries.[6] For example, with respect to telecommunications, it has been argued that the telecommunications system is a fundamental part of Canadian industrial infrastructure and therefore foreign ownership should not be permitted. (The same argument has been made with respect to the

[6] Globerman also provides a summary of the existing foreign ownership restrictions in the financial services, oil and gas, telecommunications, transportation, and agriculture industries.

transportation and financial services industries.) It has also been suggested that foreign ownership of Canadian telecommunications might endanger national defense, and that using the telecommunication and transportation sectors as instruments of industrial and regional development might be less effective under foreign ownership. In terms of foreign ownership of financial institutions, concern has been expressed regarding the possible loss of credit creation and allocation, and regarding some possible reduction in financial capital made available to domestic companies by foreign-controlled financial institutions.

Globerman (p. 23) finds that on the basis of theoretical considerations, there is no compelling welfare economics case to be made in support of general restrictions on foreign direct investment in various industries. He also finds, however, that the empirical evidence on the consequences of foreign ownership restrictions in individual industrial sectors is extremely sparse. He goes on to conclude that if non-economic considerations are motivating the maintenance of sectoral restrictions on foreign direct investment, then studies focused on the potential consequences of these restrictions are relevant.[7]

With respect to the economic effects of foreign ownership in Canada, McFetridge (1986, p. 22) cites some empirical work by Baldwin and Gorecki (1986) that has found that sub-optimal plant scale and excessive product diversity within a plant were not a consequence of foreign ownership, but rather of high tariffs in conjunction with a small domestic market.[8] Baldwin and Gorecki (1986, pp. 160–170) also found that foreign ownership did not have a negative effect on relative Canada/U.S. efficiency in the manufacturing sector; rather, if anything, it had a positive effect. Their results are in contrast to the generally mixed results found in the literature dealing with the effects of foreign ownership on productivity in Canadian manufacturing industries.[9]

It would seem then that the evidence does not support the conclusion that foreign ownership has had adverse effects on industrial performance in Canada. More research will have to be carried out, however, before the effects of foreign ownership can be known with greater certainty.

---

[7] Reproduced with permission of the Minister of Public Works and Government Services, 2004.

[8] See Chapter 2, Section V for a review of the evidence on plant scale and specialization.

[9] This literature is briefly summarized by Baldwin and Gorecki (1986, p. 163).

VI. CROWN CORPORATIONS AND MIXED ENTERPRISES

Crown corporations play an important role in Canadian industrial organization. They exist at both federal and provincial levels and they control a significant fraction of GDP, especially in certain industries (e.g., the financial industry). Borins and Boothman (1986, p.76) define Crown corporations as "wholly owned corporations either directly or indirectly, which have been formally designated as agents of the Crown for the attainment of public policy objectives, and for whose liabilities the state itself is both immediately and directly liable." Other definitions of Crown corporations have been suggested that are less restrictive in their ownership requirements.[10]

Trebilcock and Prichard (1983) have suggested seven fields of activity in which Crown corporations are observed. These are as follows:

(a) Natural monopoly regulation. As an alternative to regulating a privately-owned natural monopoly, a government may choose to own it outright. Examples are offered by provincially owned electric power utilities, such as Ontario Hydro (before restructuring in 1999) and BC Hydro.

(b) Nation building and community development. This includes infrastructure investments providing services that the private sector is unwilling to provide, and promoting Canadian nationalism. As examples, the authors suggest Canadian National Railway (before privatization), electric power utilities, Air Canada and Pacific Western Airlines (before they were privatized), and Atomic Energy of Canada Ltd.

(c) The moderation of the effects of economic transitions and the stabilization of income. This occurs, for example, when a government acquires a privately owned firm that is on the verge of bankruptcy. Examples include the Cape Breton Development Corporation, created to take over ownership of Cape Breton's coal industry and privatized in 2000, and the Canadian Saltfish Corporation, created to market saltfish (dissolved in 1995).

(d) The provision of capital funds. This occurs when there is some perceived imperfection in Canadian capital markets, when there are institutional restrictions that

---

[10] For a discussion of the problems involved in defining Crown corporations and in obtaining a comprehensive list of these corporations, see Langford and Huffman (1983).

prevent private firms from operating in a certain area of the capital market, or when the government wishes to stimulate economic activity. Crown corporations operating in this area include the Business Development Bank of Canada, Farm Credit Canada, and Export Development Canada.

(e) The promotion of national security and security of supply. Examples here include the Polymer Corporation, created in 1942 to produce synthetic rubber during World War II, and the Eldorado Mining and Refining Corporation (later called Eldorado Nuclear Ltd. and merged with the Saskatchewan Mining Development Corporation to form Cameco), acquired by the federal government in 1942 in order to supply uranium to the Manhattan Project. The authors also cite Petro-Canada as an example of a Crown corporation created (in 1975) to ensure security of supply of oil. Legislation privatizing Petro-Canada was passed in 1991.

(f) The creation of a yardstick company. This type of Crown corporation is used (i) as a source of information on a given industry and to assist in evaluating the prices, profits and performance of private firms, and (ii) to compete with private firms, particularly in markets that might be subject to collusive or anti-competitive behaviour. An example of a yardstick company was Petro-Canada before privatization.

(g) The control of externalities. The provincial liquor boards and lottery corporations are examples here.

Federal Crown Corporations

In 2002, there were 43 parent Crown corporations, and these had 21 wholly owned subsidiaries and 36 other partially owned subsidiaries, associates, and legal partnerships. As Table 1.7 shows, these numbers represent a dramatic decline from earlier years.[11] According to the Treasury Board (1992, 2003), employment in Crown corporations declined from about 207,000 in 1984–85 to 121,000 in 1991–92 and 71,165 in 2001–02. This decline is thought to be the result of both privatization and operational efficiencies.

---

[11] Figures for 1992 and 2002 are from the Treasury Board (1992, 2003), while the 1983 figures are Treasury Board figures cited in Elford and Stanbury (1986).

Table 1.7
Federal Crown Corporation Holdings, by Category

Category	1983	1992	2002
Parent Crown Corporations	67	55	43
Wholly Owned Subsidiaries	128	59	21
Other Subsidiaries, Associates, and Legal Partnerships	94	48	36

Sources: *Crown Corporations and Other Corporate Interests of Canada: Annual Report to Parliament (2002)*, p. 24, 2003, Treasury Board of Canada Secretariat. Reproduced with the permission of the Minister of Public Works and Government Services Canada, 2004.

Crown Corporations and Other Corporate Interests of Canada: Annual Report to Parliament (1991–92), p. I-27, 1992, Treasury Board of Canada Secretariat. Reproduced with the permission of the Minister of Public Works and Government Services Canada, 2004.

Federal Crown corporations fall under 10 ministerial portfolios. The Treasury Board (2003) lists these (with the value of their 2002 assets in parentheses) as follows: agriculture and agri-food ($8.0 billion), Canadian heritage ($2.7 billion), finance ($57.2 billion), fisheries and oceans ($26.5 million), foreign affairs ($60.6 million), industry ($7.0 billion), international trade ($24.5 billion), natural resources ($1.0 billion), public works and government services ($7.4 million), and transport ($28.8 billion). Total assets of these Crown corporations are $129.3 billion in 2001–2002, or $87.5 billion if the Bank of Canada is excluded.

Provincial Crown Corporations

Statistics Canada breaks the assets of provincial government enterprises down into nine categories. Table 1.8 provides the total national assets of each category for 2000. Electric power represents 69 percent of all assets of provincial Crown corporations, while finance, insurance, and real estate represent 22 percent.

The provincial distribution of the assets of provincial government enterprises is provided in Table 1.9. The province of Quebec represents 42 percent of provincial Crown corporation assets, while the province of Ontario has the second largest assets in provincial government enterprises, at 25 percent.

Chapter 1

Table 1.8
Distribution of Total Assets of Provincial Government Enterprises, by Industry

Function	% of Total Provincial Government Enterprise Assets
Trade	0.73
Finance, Insurance, and Real Estate	22.15
Community Businesses and Personal Services	2.90
Mines, Quarries, and Oil Wells	0.11
Manufacturing	1.19
Transportation	2.19
Communication	0.66
Electric Power	69.40
Gas Distribution	0.66

Source: Adapted from the Statistics Canada CANSIM database http://cansim2.statscan.ca, Table 385-0016. Date of extraction Jan. 15, 2004.

Table 1.9
Total Assets of Provincial Government Enterprises, by Province

Province	Total Assets of Provincial Government Enterprises ($000,000)	Percentage of Total
Quebec	83,087.1	42.7
Ontario	49,105.0	25.2
British Columbia	23,074.7	11.9
Alberta	12,034.4	6.2
Manitoba	10,420.1	5.4
Saskatchewan	8,192.9	4.2
New Brunswick	3,877.9	2.0
Newfoundland	2,359.5	1.2
Nova Scotia	1,972.6	1.0
Northwest Territories	284.6	0.1
Yukon	149.7	0.1
Prince Edward Island	82.8	0.0

Source: Adapted from the Statistics Canada CANSIM database http://cansim2.statscan.ca, Table 385-0016. Date of extraction Jan. 15, 2004.

Other Corporate Interests of Canada and the Provinces

The federal and provincial governments may own voting shares of business enterprises, along with other private shareholders, individuals, or other provincial governments. The Treasury Board (2003) divides such cases for the federal government into five categories:

(1) A *mixed enterprise* for the federal government is a corporate entity "whose shares are partially owned by Canada, through a minister. Private-sector parties own the remaining shares."

(2) A *joint enterprise* is a corporate entity "whose shares are partially owned by Canada, through a minister. The balance of shares is owned by another level of government."

(3) Canada may hold shares in *international organizations* created under international agreements, or have the right to appoint or elect members of the governing body.

(4) A *shared-governance corporation* is a corporate entity "without share capital for which Canada, either directly or through a Crown corporation, has a right … to appoint or nominate one or more members to the governing body."

(5) Finally, Canada may own shares of a corporate entity under the terms of the *Bankruptcy and Insolvency Act.*

According to the Treasury Board (2003), the only mixed enterprise as of July 31, 2002, was Petro-Canada, of which the federal government owned 18.84 percent. There were three joint enterprises, with the provinces of Quebec, Manitoba, and Newfoundland. Canada had interests in 18 international organizations and 139 shared-governance corporations, and owned shares of 25 firms under the *Bankruptcy and Insolvency Act.* No similar statistics are available for the provinces.

Crown Corporations and Economic Efficiency

Given the historical economic significance of public enterprises in Canada, economists have dedicated considerable attention to the relative efficiency of Crown corporations and private sector firms. Surveys of this literature have been completed by McFetridge

(1997) and Borins and Boothman (1986). Borins and Boothman review studies that have compared Canadian National (at the time a federal Crown corporation) with Canadian Pacific, Air Canada (before it was privatized) with Canadian Pacific and other private Canadian and American airlines, as well as private firms with Crown corporations in the bus transportation, telecommunications, electricity provision, steel, and oil industries. Their conclusion (on page 121) was that "There is no consistent evidence demonstrating that public enterprise is inherently less efficient than private enterprise." Furthermore, they found that "performance is conditional upon the intensity and form of competition and regulation and upon the monitoring and incentive systems under which public enterprise managers work."

McFetridge (1997) considered studies examined by Borin and Boothman as well as more recent studies comparing government enterprises and private firms in Canada and other countries. He concluded that comparisons of government enterprises and private firms yield little convincing evidence that private enterprises are more productive or efficient than public enterprises.

Privatization

Privatization of Crown corporations has been a prominent feature of the federal government's economic policy since the mid 1980s. Stanbury (1994) reported that between 1983 and September of 1994, the federal government sold all or substantially all of the shares in 15 Crown corporations, while there were 20 such transactions by provincial governments. Including sales of shares in mixed enterprises or limited assets of Crown corporations, Stanbury concluded that there were 28 federal privatization transactions over this period, and 74 transactions at the provincial level.

Levac and Wooldridge (1997) reported that the 10 largest federal privatizations over the 1986–1996 period, listed in Table 1.10, earned sales proceeds of $7.218 billion. Of these 10 transactions, four were in the transportation sector; these four transactions represented sales proceeds of $4.194 billion. In contrast, Table 1.11 indicates that over the period 1990–1995, the largest provincial and municipal privatizations were in the communications sector, with three transactions accounting for $3.063 billion. Of the nine largest provincial and municipal privatizations over this period, four were in the province of Alberta.

Table 1.10
Largest Privatizations of Federal Crown Corporations, 1986–1996

Name	Sector	Year	Sale Proceeds ($000,000)
Canadian National Railway Co.	Transportation	1995	2,079
Petro-Canada	Oil and gas	1991	1,747
Nav Canada	Transportation	1996	1,500
Air Canada	Transportation	1988	474
Teleglobe Canada	Telecommunications	1987	441
Canada Development Corporation	Financial	1987	365
Nordion International	Manufacturing	1991	161
Telesat Canada	Telecommunications	1992	155
de Havilland Inc.	Manufacturing	1986	155
Canadair	Transportation	1986	141

Source: Levac and Wooldridge (1997).

Table 1.11
Largest Privatizations of Provincial and Municipal Crown Corporations, 1990–1995

Name	Sector	Year	Sale Proceeds ($000,000)
Alberta Government Telephones	Telecommunications	1990	1,735
Manitoba Telephone Systems	Telecommunications	1996	860
Cameco	Mining	1991	855
Nova Scotia Power Corp.	Electricity Generation	1992	816
Syncrude Canada	Oil and Gas	1993	502
Edmonton Telephones	Telecommunications	1995	468
Potash Corp. of Saskatchewan	Mining	1989	388
Suncor	Oil and Gas	1992	299
Vencap Equities Alberta	Financial	1995	174

Source: Levac and Wooldridge (1997).

Dalfen (1990) has summarized the federal government's stated reasons for privatizing Crown corporations as follows:

(a) The disappearance of the original objectives of a Crown corporation due to a changing economic environment; or alternatively, the emergence of taxation, spending and/or regulation as more valid options to ownership.
(b) The increased efficiency resulting from placing a Crown corporation within the test of the marketplace.
(c) The great demand that public ownership places upon government resources to properly manage and support these undertakings on a day-to-day basis.
(d) The inability of Crown corporations to properly adjust to changes in markets and/or technologies due to the slow and deliberate decision making which is inherent in the operation of a business using the taxpayers' money.
(e) The inappropriateness of Crown corporations competing head-to-head with one or more entities in the private sector.[12]

A detailed discussion of the efficiency rationale for privatization is provided by McFetridge (1997). McFetridge identifies several ways in which privatization may increase efficiency. First, an enterprise may operate more efficiently under private ownership because of profit incentives to increase the enterprise's value. Support for this hypothesis is provided by Boardman et al. (2002), who examine the operating and stock price performance of major Canadian privatizations, and conclude that privatization has improved the operating and financial performance of these companies. In addition, an enterprise may be operated inefficiently for political reasons. McFetridge provides the example of government-owned utilities which over invest in capacity because consumers will likely punish the government politically for service interruptions. Third, McFetridge considers whether privatization of a Crown corporation could increase the efficiency of the market. It is unclear, however, whether competition in a market would be increased by privatizing one of the firms operating in the market. Finally, privatization may increase the efficiency of the political system by removing the operation of government enterprises from the political agenda.

---

[12] Dalfen (1990) found these reasons stated in a document issued on May 1, 1987, by the Ministry of State for Privatization and entitled "Excerpts from Statements Made by the Honourable Barbara McDougall on the Reasons for Privatization."

While there are several ways in which privatization may increase efficiency, it does not follow that efficiency will increase in all cases. McFetridge (1997, p. 2) explains that "Not all experiments with privatization have been economically successful. Nor should we expect them to be." Therefore, whether privatization is likely to increase efficiency will depend upon the specific circumstances of each case and the way in which the privatization is carried out.

Privatization of Liquor Retailing in Alberta

As an example of what some economists would regard as a successful privatization, consider the privatization of liquor retailing in Alberta, which occurred in September 1993. Prior to that date, liquor stores in Alberta, as in other provinces in Canada, were owned and operated by the provincial government. There were few government-owned liquor stores in Alberta: 24 in Calgary, 23 in Edmonton, and 158 in the rest of the province. All government liquor stores charged the same prices, and carried a relatively restricted variety of products. According to West (2003), the Alberta Liquor Control Board (ALCB) had 1,957 catalogue listings in September 1993, and 1,221 listings as part of the Agents' Listing Program. An ALCB store would stock between 600 and 2600 products, depending on the store type. Liquor stores were unionized. The government charged an ad valorem markup on the wholesale price of liquor products, and liquor stores returned a gross profit of about $492 million in the fiscal year ending January 5, 1993.

Privatization of liquor retailing allowed a large number of liquor stores to be opened across the province. By December 2001, there were 207 liquor stores in Calgary, 156 in Edmonton, and 495 in the rest of Alberta. Liquor stores were permitted to set their own prices, but the wholesale prices were still set by the government through the Alberta Liquor Control Board (ALCB), superseded by the Alberta Gaming and Liquor Commission (AGLC). There is some evidence that the average real retail price of liquor products increased modestly after privatization (about 4 percent between October 1993 and January 1996), and this could be partly due to the double markups to which liquor products were now subject.[13] However, the larger number of liquor stores would also help consumers reduce the transportation and shopping costs incurred to purchase liquor products.

---

[13] See Carlton and Perloff (2004), Chapter 12 for a discussion of the double marginalization problem. See also West (2000) for a discussion of double marginalization and privatization in liquor retailing.

The product variety from which liquor stores can choose to serve their customers has increased dramatically: during the 12 months prior to August 31, 2002, there were 25,305 different products that moved through the government's liquor warehouse, and 10,959 of these products were stocked in the warehouse on August 31, 2002. Liquor store employment has increased substantially since privatization, although at much reduced wages. West (2003) found that in February 1996, the average wage paid by private liquor stores was $7.19, about half the wage paid by the ALCB to liquor store clerks at the top of the union scale. At the time of privatization, the government changed its liquor markup from a set of ad valorem markups to a set of flat markups on liquor products. In the fiscal year ending March 31, 2001, the Government of Alberta still received gross profits of about $468 million on liquor sales. These gross profits would return a higher net profit under privatization than under government ownership of liquor stores because the costs of owning and operating liquor stores are no longer deducted from gross profits. Privatization per se need not imply any reduction in government revenues from the sale of liquor products.[14]

Alberta's experience with the privatization of liquor retailing has been studied by a number of provincial governments. Retailing, it might be argued, is not an activity in which government has any particular expertise or public need in pursuing. However, even while the consumer benefits of privatized liquor retailing (e.g., closer liquor store locations on average, greater product variety, price competition) would seem to be compelling, one must still compare the benefits with the costs of privatization (e.g., the costs of operating what could be an excessive number of stores). One might also wish to consider whether privatization of liquor retailing would result in an increase in social costs (e.g., minors obtaining easier access to beverage alcohol). A complete cost/benefit analysis of the privatization of liquor retailing has yet to be carried out.

VII. INTERNATIONAL TRADE IN CANADA

Economists usually regard Canada as having a small open economy. This is because Canada's economy is about one-tenth the size of the U.S. economy, and the value of exports and imports is large relative to GDP. Table 1.12 contains some recent data on

---

[14] See West (2003) for a more complete presentation of the statistics related to Alberta's liquor store privatization, as well as a discussion of the economic impacts of the privatization of liquor stores in Alberta.

Table 1.12
Exports and Imports from Principal Trading Areas (Customs Basis), 2000–2002

	Year	Total Domestic Exports ($000,000)	Total Domestic Imports ($000,000)
U.S.	2000	334,145.7	229,658.1
	2001	325,034.2	218,407.9
	2002	317,990.5	218,162.7
Mexico	2000	1,940.4	12,067.2
	2001	2,352.4	12,109.9
	2002	2,274.8	12,702.6
Japan	2000	9,074.2	16,608.7
	2001	8,067.0	14,646.8
	2002	8,190.8	15,406.0
EU	2000	18,304.7	36,907.2
	2001	17,244.6	38,399.8
	2002	16,112.9	38,955.1
Other Countries	2000	16,823.5	48,623.9
	2001	16,526.4	48,115.9
	2002	16,046.9	52,136.9
Total	2000	385,363.7	356,851.4
	2001	373,554.2	343,055.6
	2002	365,139.7	348,444.6

Source: Adapted from the Statistics Canada publication *Canadian International Merchandise Trade*, Catalogue 65-001, Vol. 56, Issue 12, Dec. 2001, p. 13, and Vol. 57, Issue 12, Dec. 2002, p. 15.

total domestic exports and imports in 2000, 2001, and 2002 by trading area. The U.S. is the largest of Canada's trading partners, accounting for 87 percent of Canada's exports and 63 percent of Canada's imports in 2002. The European Union accounted for 4 percent of exports and 11 percent of imports, while Japan accounted for 2 percent of exports and 4 percent of imports, and Mexico accounted for one-half a percent of exports and 4 percent of imports. The value of total exports relative to GDP (at market prices) in 2002 was 0.36, while the value of imports relative to GDP (at market prices) was 0.31. The U.S. took a larger fraction of Canadian exports (87 percent) than it had in 1960 (56 percent), 1970 (65 percent), and 1992 (77 percent). The increase in exports to the U.S. in the 1960s is partly due to the introduction of the Auto Pact, while the recent increase in exports is likely due to the Free Trade Agreement with the U.S. that went into effect in 1989, and the North American Free Trade Agreement (NAFTA), which came into effect in 1994.

Before the Free Trade agreement with the U.S. and its successor, NAFTA, the Economic Council of Canada (1983) found that nominal and effective tariffs in Canada had been falling from 11.9 and 16.4 percent, respectively, in 1966 to 7.8 and 11.7 percent, respectively, in 1978. Imports not subject to tariffs had increased from 35.4 percent of total imports in 1970 to 45.9 percent of total imports in 1979. In 1987, prior to the signing of the Free Trade Agreement, more than 75 percent of trade between Canada and the U.S. was free of duty.[15]

The Canada-U.S. Free Trade Agreement committed the two countries to eliminating all tariffs on manufacturing within 10 years. Some tariffs were eliminated immediately after the Agreement went into effect, some were to be eliminated in five equal steps, and other tariffs were to be eliminated in 10 equal steps. This agreement was strengthened by the North American Free Trade Agreement, which came into effect in 1994 and included Mexico. Under the Canada-U.S. Free Trade Agreement, import or export quotas were to be eliminated, either immediately or according to a timetable. Canada and the U.S. agreed to avoid the use of standard-related measures as unnecessary obstacles to trade. The Agreement did not affect the ability of the federal and provincial governments to operate programs that protect and stabilize farm incomes. The Agreement secured Canada's access to the U.S. market for energy goods. The Auto Pact safeguards remain largely intact.

The Canada-U.S. Free Trade Agreement covered most commercial services. Canada and the U.S. agreed to extend the principle of national treatment to the providers of certain services and they agreed not to discriminate between Canadian and American providers of these services. Each country remains free to choose whether to regulate services and how to regulate. The Agreement sought to relax restrictions on U.S. investment in Canada and Canadian investment in the U.S., and it raised the threshold at which a U.S. acquisition of a Canadian firm would be reviewed by Investment Canada to $150 million. The Agreement also contained a dispute settlement mechanism and special arrangements for dealing with antidumping and countervailing duties.

---

[15] See External Affairs Canada (1987, p. 18).

Chapter 1

In the decades before the Free Trade agreement came into effect, economists had argued that the tariff could be one of the important causes of inefficiency in production in Canada. Eastman and Stykolt (1967, p. 7) advanced the theory that "excess costs of production are the consequence of excess tariff protection. With lower protection Canadian plants with excess costs would be obliged to lower costs in order to survive against foreign competition; they would be larger and fewer." Harris (1984) characterized the industrial organization approach to trade as having the view that "protection, by restricting market size and limiting foreign competition, promotes too many small firms within an industry, operating at too small a scale, and with too many product lines being produced within the plant. Related is the observation that protection may facilitate oligopolistic coordination of the protected firms." Furthermore, if Canada's trading partners also have tariffs, it makes it more difficult for Canadian producers to reach minimum efficient scale by exporting.

The studies cited above do tend to suggest that the reduction of trade barriers between Canada and other countries should result in fairly impressive efficiency gains. An opportunity to evaluate the actual results of reduced trade barriers has been created by the implementation of the Canada-U.S. Free Trade Agreement and NAFTA. Trefler (2001) reported that Canada's average tariff rate in manufacturing against the United States fell from 5.6 percent in 1988 before the Free Trade Agreement, to 1.0 percent by 1996.

Several recent studies have examined the impact of the Free Trade Agreement on different aspects of the Canadian economy. Trefler (2001) conducted an empirical analysis of the short- and long-term effects of the Free Trade Agreement on manufacturing industries. Trefler concluded that:

(a) For manufacturing as a whole, tariff cuts reduced employment by 5 percent, output by 3 percent, and the number of plants by 4 percent over the 1988–1996 period, although since 1996 output and employment have largely rebounded. These numbers are associated with the large transition costs of reallocating resources from heavily protected industries.

(b) The tariff cuts increased labour productivity by a compounded annual rate of 0.6 percent, and increased total factor productivity by a compounded annual rate of 0.2

percent for manufacturing as a whole. These increases are associated with plant turnover and increased technical efficiency within plants.

As a general comment, Trefler argues on page 38 that "most of the effects of the FTA tariff cuts are smaller than one would imagine given the heat generated by the debate."

VIII. SUMMARY

In this chapter, the economic context within which firms in Canada operate and compete has been reviewed. It began with a description of the industrial composition of GDP and the size distribution of manufacturing industries in Canada. Some data on Canadian corporate size were then presented which indicate that Canadian corporations are not large relative to corporations in the rest of the world. This was followed by a discussion of aggregate corporate concentration in Canada. Historically, the data showed that aggregate concentration was higher in Canada than in the U.S. The small size of Canada's domestic market was thought to be partly responsible for this result. The promotion of larger Canadian firms so that scale economies could be realised was one of the principal motivations of the Free Trade Agreement with the U.S.

The extent of foreign ownership of Canadian industry was described, and it was shown that foreign-controlled revenues as a share of total Canadian revenues increased in the 1980s. The U.S. holds the largest share of foreign-controlled assets and revenues in Canada. The available evidence does not support the conclusion that foreign ownership has had adverse effects on industrial performance in Canada.

A description of Crown corporation involvement in the Canadian economy was presented next. The number of federal Crown corporations has been decreasing in the 1980s and 1990s, and this has been largely due to privatization. Provincial Crown corporations are particularly important in the utility sector of the economy. Quebec has the largest share of provincial Crown corporation assets at 42 percent, while Ontario has the second largest share at 25 percent. The increasing importance of privatization of Crown corporations was also discussed.

Finally, the importance of international trade to the Canadian economy, and the effects of the tariff on Canadian manufacturing industries were discussed. Studies done prior to the implementation of the FTA or NAFTA suggested that some fairly impressive efficiency gains would be one of the outcomes of the reduction of trade barriers between Canada and the U.S. The empirical literature has confirmed that there have been positive gains from the implementation of the FTA and NAFTA.

REFERENCES

Baldwin, John R. and Paul K. Gorecki. 1986. *The Role of Scale in Canada–U.S. Productivity Differences in the Manufacturing Sector, 1970–1979*. Toronto: University of Toronto Press.

Boardman, Anthony E., Claude Laurin, and Aidan R. Vining. 2002. "Privatization in Canada: Operating and Stock Price Performance with International Comparisons," *Canadian Journal of Administrative Sciences* 19: 137–154.

Borins, Sanford F. and Barry E.C. Boothman. 1986. "Crown Corporations and Economic Efficiency," in Donald G. McFetridge, ed., *Canadian Industrial Policy in Action*. Toronto: University of Toronto Press.

Carlton, Dennis W. and Jeffrey M. Perloff. 2004. *Modern Industrial Organization*, Fourth Edition. New York: Pearson Education.

Dalfen, Charles.1990. "Deregulation and Privatization in the Canadian Telecommunications Sector: The Case of Teleglobe Canada," in Jeremy Richardson, ed., *Privatisation and Deregulation in Canada and Britain*. Aldershot: Dartmouth Publishing Co.

Eastman, H.C. and S. Stykolt. 1967. *The Tariff and Competition in Canada*. Toronto: Macmillan.

Economic Council of Canada. 1983. *The Bottom Line: Technology, Trade and Income Growth*. Ottawa: Minister of Supply and Services Canada.

Elford, E. Craig and W.T. Stanbury. 1986. "Mixed Enterprises in Canada," in Donald G. McFetridge, ed., *Canadian Industry in Transition*. Toronto: University of Toronto Press.

External Affairs Canada. 1987. *The Canada–U.S. Free Trade Agreement Synopsis*.

Globerman, S. 1999. "Implications of Foreign Ownership Restrictions for the Canadian Economy—A Sectoral Analysis," Industry Canada Discussion Paper No. 7, April 1999.

Harris, Richard. 1984. "Applied General Equilibrium Analysis of Small Open Economies with Scale Economies and Imperfect Competition," *American Economic Review* 74: 1016–1032.

Langford, John W. and Kenneth J. Huffman. 1983. "The Uncharted Universe of Federal Public Corporations," in J. Robert S. Prichard, ed., *Crown Corporations in Canada*. Toronto: Butterworths.

Levac, Mylene and Philip Wooldridge. 1997. "The Fiscal Impact of Privatization in Canada," *Bank of Canada Review*, 25–40.

McFetridge, Donald G. 1986. "The Economics of Industrial Structure: An Overview," in Donald G. McFetridge, ed., *Canadian Industry in Transition*. Toronto: University of Toronto Press.

McFetridge, Donald G. 1997. "The Economics of Privatization," C.D. Howe Institute Benefactors Lecture.

Royal Commission on Corporate Concentration. 1978. *Report of the Royal Commission on Corporate Concentration*. Ottawa: Minister of Supply and Services Canada.

Stanbury, William T. 1994. "The Extent of Privatization in Canada: 1979–1994." Paper presented at the Canadian Law and Economics Association meetings, University of Toronto, Faculty of Law, September 30–October 1.

Statistics Canada. 1991. *Corporations and Labour Unions Returns Act, Part 1: Corporations*, Report for 1988, Cat. No. 61-210. Ottawa: Minister of Industry, Science and Technology.

Statistics Canada. 2001. *Corporations Returns Act*, Report for 1998, Cat. No. 61-220-XPB, Ottawa: Minister of Industry.

Statistics Canada. 2003. *Corporations Returns Act*, Report for 2000, Cat. No. 61-220-XIE, Ottawa: Minister of Industry.

Treasury Board of Canada. 1992. *Crown Corporations and Other Corporate Interests of Canada 1991-92*. Ottawa: Minister of Supply and Services Canada.

Treasury Board of Canada. 2003. *2002 Annual Report to Parliament – Crown Corporations and Other Corporate Interests of Canada*. Ottawa: Canadian Government Publishing.

Trebilcock, M.J. and J.R.S. Prichard. 1983. "Crown Corporations: The Calculus of Instrument Choice," in J. Robert S. Prichard, ed., *Crown Corporations in Canada*. Toronto: Butterworths.

Trefler, D. 2001. "The Long and The Short of the Canada–U.S. Free Trade Agreement," NBER Working Paper No. 8293.

West, Douglas S. 2000. "Double Marginalization and Privatization in Liquor Retailing," *Review of Industrial Organization* 16: 399–415.

West, Douglas S. 2003. *The Privatization of Liquor Retailing in Alberta*. Fraser Institute Digital Publication. Vancouver: The Fraser Institute.

Williamson, Oliver E. 1968. "Economies as an Antitrust Defense: The Welfare Tradeoffs," *American Economic Review* 58: 18–34.

CHAPTER 2

CANADIAN MARKET STRUCTURE, MERGER ACTIVITY, ENTRY/EXIT ACTIVITY, AND INDUSTRIAL PERFORMANCE

I. INTRODUCTION

In this chapter, a more detailed examination is made of Canadian market structure and the entry/exit and merger activity that affect that structure. First, measures of concentration are reported for a sample of Canadian industries. Next, merger activity in Canada is reviewed along with some results on the outcomes of that activity. This is followed by a review of the evidence regarding scale economies in Canadian manufacturing industry and the evidence on the specialization of production in Canadian plants. Some results on entry into and exit from Canadian manufacturing industries are then discussed. Finally, results obtained in Canadian studies of market structure and industrial performance are briefly summarized.

Since the late 1980s, there have been significant developments (and attempted developments) in market structure in three key Canadian industries: the oil industry, the airline industry, and the banking industry. Some of these developments will be summarized below, as they will help to illustrate the importance of the market structure characteristics that economists typically examine in competition cases.

II. CONCENTRATION IN CANADIAN INDUSTRY

Concentration in Canadian industry has been calculated using the four-firm and eight-firm concentration ratios for the year 1988. An n-firm industry concentration ratio measures the percentage of industry sales accounted for by the largest firms in the industry.[1] While these statistics tell us something about industrial concentration, they do not convey reliable information regarding the nature of competition in a relevant market.[2] This is because the available measures of concentration have been calculated for two-digit Standard Industrial Classification (SIC) industries, and these industries do not constitute relevant markets for competition analysis. The industries are too broadly defined, and concentration measures for these industries are only available for Canada as

---

[1] Measures of concentration are discussed in Chapter 8 of Carlton and Perloff (2004).

[2] An economic market consists of a set of competing products, a set of buyers, a set of sellers, and a geographic area in which competition occurs that determines the price(s) for the products in the market.

a whole (whereas markets might be local in nature).[3]

Table 2.1 presents a broad picture of concentration in two-digit SIC industries in Canada in 1988. Some industries, such as tobacco products and petroleum and coal products, were relatively concentrated even at this level, while others, such as construction, services, wholesale trade, and retail trade, were not. The transportation and finance industries had modest four-firm concentration ratios of 36.4 and 16.4 percent, respectively, but these figures understate the extent of concentration in particular segments of these industries.

For example, in the banking industry, there are only five banks with a national presence (i.e., Bank of Montreal, CIBC, Royal Bank, TD, and Scotiabank), several banks with a regional presence (e.g., National Bank, Hongkong Bank of Canada, Alberta Treasury Branches), and credit unions that offer a limited range of financial products and services.[4] Market shares are only meaningfully calculated for relevant product and geographic markets within which banks compete. In its 1998 review of the proposed merger between CIBC and TD and the proposed merger between Royal Bank and Bank of Montreal, the Competition Bureau defined a number of relevant product markets (related to branch banking, credit cards, and securities). It found, partly on the basis of market share calculations, that the proposed merger between CIBC and TD would result in a substantial lessening of competition (SLC) in 36 of 179 local markets for branch banking services, and might result in an SLC in another 53 local markets.[5] The proposed merger was also found to result in an SLC in the Visa merchant acquiring market (the business of providing settlement of Visa credit card transactions to merchants), and in one of 22 local markets in which CIBC Wood Gundy and TD Evergreen compete in full-service brokerage services. The proposed merger between Royal Bank and Bank of

---

[3] The Standard Industrial Classification, replaced by the North American Industry Classification System in 1997, is the basic way of classifying firms on the basis of the outputs they produce.

[4] Baltazar and Santos (2003) report that of the 54 banks in Canada that accounted for combined assets of over $1.4 trillion, the top five banks made up over 80 percent of total industry assets.

[5] According to the *Enforcement Guidelines on the Abuse of Dominance Provisions* issued by the Competition Bureau in July 2001 (page 3), the meaning of preventing or lessening competition substantially has been established in case law. "The question is whether the anti-competitive acts engaged in by a firm or group of firms serve to preserve, entrench or enhance their market power," including the ability to raise price profitably above competitive levels for a considerable period of time.

Table 2.1

Concentration Ratios in Selected Industries, 1988

Industry	Percent of Revenue Controlled by Leading Enterprises	
	CR4	CR8
Tobacco products	98.9	100.0
Petroleum and coal products	74.5	90.8
Storage	71.7	79.0
Beverages	59.2	77.6
Primary metals	63.3	76.6
Communications/	64.8	76.4
Rubber products	51.2	74.5
Transport equipment	68.4	74.4
Public utilities	58.4	73.9
Metal mining	58.9	73.0
Mineral fuels	38.6	54.4
Paper and allied industries	38.9	52.6
Non-metallic mineral products	30.6	44.1
Transportation	36.4	43.3
Electrical products	32.1	40.9
Textile mills	32.5	40.9
Printing, publishing and allied industries	25.7	37.4
Chemicals and chemical products	25.5	35.4
Finance	16.4	28.9
Food	19.6	28.7
Leather products	16.9	26.2
Wood industries	17.8	25.2
Other mining	14.1	21.9
Knitting mills	11.4	21.5
Machinery	11.3	18.6
Metal fabricating	11.4	18.1
Retail trade	9.7	14.8
Miscellaneous manufacturing	10.2	14.2
Furniture industries	7.6	13.4
Wholesale trade	7.4	12.5
Clothing industries	6.6	9.9
Services	4.5	6.9
Agriculture, forestry, fishing	2.6	4.4
Construction	2.2	3.5

Source: Adapted from the Statistics Canada publication *Annual Report of the Minister of Industry, Science and Technology under the Corporations and Labour Union Returns Act* (CALURA), *Part I, Corporations, 1988*, Catalogue 61-210, October, 1991, Table 5.4, p. 94.

Montreal was similarly found to result in an SLC in certain branch banking, credit card and securities markets.[6]

The low four-firm concentration ratio (CR4) for the finance industry as a whole would not have suggested that a merger in this industry would likely result in an SLC. As another example, in the Canadian airline industry in 1998, Air Canada and Canadian Airlines accounted for 90 percent of the total domestic passenger revenues.[7] This is in contrast to the four-firm transportation industry concentration ratio of 36.4 percent. In the petroleum industry, concentration and market shares are again only meaningfully calculated for relevant product and geographic markets. In the petroleum industry, there will be different markets defined at the crude oil production, refining and refined product distribution levels. For example, retail gasoline markets are local in nature. Market shares and concentration levels will vary by market, depending on the extent to which national refiners, regional refiners, and independent retailers own gas stations in the local market.

Baldwin and Gorecki (1991a) calculated the ratio of CR4 in 1979 to CR4 in 1970 for 167 four-digit manufacturing industries, and found that the variable was centred on one, and had a mean of 1.0007. The mean (over the 167 four-digit industries) proportion of industry shipments accounted for by the leading four firms declined from 50.9 percent in 1970 to 49.9 percent in 1979, suggesting relative stability in industrial concentration during this period. Baldwin and Gorecki believed that the relative stability of market structure conveyed by concentration ratios masks important changes that occur in the number and size distribution of firms and identity of leading firms. Their investigations of firm mobility and entry and exit will be discussed in Section VI.

---

[6] See the letters from Konrad von Finckenstein, Commissioner of Competition, to CIBC and TD Banks, and Royal Bank and Bank of Montreal, dated December 11, 1998, available on the Competition Bureau's website at http://www.competition.ic.gc.ca.

[7] The remaining revenues were accounted for by WestJet and four charter carriers, Air Transat, Canada 3000, Royal Airlines, and SkyService. See the letter from Konrad von Finckenstein, Commissioner of Competition, to David Collenette, Minister of Transport, available on the Competition Bureau's website, www.competition.ic.gc.ca.

III. MERGERS

Merger activity can have important long-run effects on the market structures faced by Canadian firms, particularly if the mergers are horizontal in nature. Horizontal mergers will increase concentration in the market in which the merging firms compete.[8]

Table 2.2 presents merger examination data compiled by the Canadian Competition Bureau. The Bureau is responsible for enforcement of the *Competition Act,* which contains a number of provisions dealing with mergers. The Act requires that the Bureau receive notification of mergers of a certain size, and these are the mergers whose outcomes are summarized in Table 2.2.[9]

Note first that there is a relatively small number of mergers reviewed in 1986–87 because the data are not for a complete fiscal year, and the *Competition Act,* with its new merger review provisions, was only passed in June of 1986. The number of merger examinations commenced was more or less increasing from 1986 to 1998, and reached a peak in 1999–2000 with 425 merger examinations commenced, but then declined over the next three years. The decline in merger activity coincided with the slowdown in economic activity that began in 2001. As row 2 of the table shows, most merger examinations commenced by the Bureau were concluded as posing no competition issue under the Act. On some occasions, the Bureau negotiates with the parties to a merger to resolve competition concerns, and this can result in either pre- or post-closing restructuring (rows 4 and 5) of the merger (e.g., asset divestitures). On rare occasions, the Bureau will negotiate an agreement with the parties to a merger and ask the Competition Tribunal (a court of record responsible for hearing applications brought to it under Part VIII of the Act, which includes the merger provisions) to issue a consent order approving the agreement. Also on rare occasions, the Bureau will file an application with the Tribunal, opposing a proposed merger.

Since 1989, the Competition Bureau has reviewed large proposed mergers in the oil industry, banking industry, and airline industry. In 1989, Imperial Oil Limited sought to acquire Texaco Canada Inc. The merger would reduce the number of national vertically integrated oil companies from four to three, and make Imperial Oil the largest gasoline

---

[8] Carlton and Perloff (2004) discuss merger activity and effects in Chapter 2.

[9] See Chapter 4 for a more detailed discussion of merger policy in Canada and the notification provisions of the *Competition Act.*

Table 2.2
Merger Examinations under the Competition Act

	1986 =87[1]	1989 =90	1992 =93	1995 =96	1998 =99	2002 =03
Merger Examinations Commenced[2]	40	219	204	228	361	279
Examinations Concluded						
Concluded as posing no issue under the *Act*	17	204	198	204	346	257
Concluded with monitoring only	5	13	4	4	-	-
Concluded with pre-closing restructuring	-	-	-	-	-	{ 6
Concluded with post-closing restructuring	1	1	-	-	1	
Concluded with Consent Order	-	3	-	-	2	3
Parties abandoned proposed merger in whole or in part as a result of Director's position	3	2	3	3	3	-
Total Examinations Concluded	26	223	207	215	354	267
Examinations Ongoing at End of Period	14	31	31	52	47	27
Applications Before Tribunal						
Concluded[3]	1	3	2	1	4	1
Ongoing	-	1	1	2	1	4

[1]Statistics commenced on June 19, 1986. [2]Two or more days of review. [3]These matters are counted under examinations concluded.

Source: *Annual Reports of the Director of Investigation and Research, Competition Act, for the Years Ending March 31, 1988; March 31, 1990; March 31, 1993. Annual Reports of the Commissioner of Competition, Competition Act, for the Years Ending March 31, 2000; March 31, 2003. Competition Bureau Annual Report for the Year Ending March 31, 1997.* Reproduced with the permission of the Minister of Public Works and Government Services, 2004.

retailer in most areas of Canada. It would also solidify its position as the largest refiner in Canada. This proposed merger was subject to extensive review by the Bureau, and negotiations with the parties to the merger to resolve competition concerns. Ultimately, the Competition Tribunal approved a consent order requiring asset divestitures and supply assurances (i.e., that the merged firm will continue to make gasoline supplies available to independent gas stations).

In 1998, two large bank mergers were proposed: the Bureau was notified of the proposed merger between Royal Bank and Bank of Montreal in January 1998, and the proposed merger between CIBC and TD Bank in April 1998. After reviewing these mergers, the Bureau summarized its findings in two letters, dated December 11, 1998, to the Royal Bank/Bank of Montreal and CIBC/TD Banks. It found that the mergers would result in a substantial lessening of competition in certain markets. However, the banks did not have an opportunity to negotiate asset divestitures to resolve the competition concerns as the Minister of Finance rejected the proposed mergers on December 14, 1998.

In 1999, Canada's largest air carrier, Air Canada, proposed taking over Canada's second largest air carrier, Canadian Airlines Corporation. While the Bureau believed that the merger would raise significant competition concerns, it also concluded that the proposed transaction, subject to some undertakings, was preferable to the liquidation of Canadian due to its imminent insolvency.[10] The undertakings required Air Canada to allow small Canadian carriers to participate in its Aeroplan frequent flyer program, placed delays on Air Canada's operation of a discount carrier in Eastern Canada, required that Air Canada give up some slots at Toronto's Lester B. Pearson International Airport, and required the divestiture of its regional carrier, CRAL.

The mergers, both proposed and completed, in the oil, banking, and airline industries involved the largest firms operating in those industries, and could clearly have had significant market structure, competition, and welfare implications. They may or may not have led to substantial gains for the merging parties, depending on how the market values the likely future outcomes resulting from the merger.

One question then that naturally arises when examining mergers is whether or not both parties to a merger participate in the merger's gains. Carlton and Perloff (2004, Chapter 2) summarize the results from a number of studies that have considered this question. Here, the results of Eckbo's (1986, 1988) and Eckbo and Thorburn's (2000) studies of Canadian mergers will be summarized.

---

[10] The undertakings that Air Canada accepted are contained in a letter from the Competition Bureau to Lawson Hunter of Stikeman Elliott, dated December 21, 1999, and the letter is available on the Competition Bureau's website at www.competition.ic.gc.ca.

Chapter 2

Eckbo was interested in estimating the valuation effects of corporate acquisitions in Canada. His study can be classified as an "event" study of mergers since he wanted to find the effect that the announcement of a merger (the "event") had on the rate of return of the bidder (or acquiring) firm and the target (or acquired) firm. For this purpose, Eckbo used the *Merger Register* that was maintained by the Department of Consumer and Corporate Affairs Canada to obtain information on the bidder and target firms involved in mergers, the newspaper in which the merger was announced and a short summary of the major activity of the two firms involved in the merger. There were 7,559 acquisition bids reported in the *Merger Register* for the sample period 1964–1983, but only 1,930 of these were included in the sample because Eckbo's analysis required share price information and the returns for either the target or bidder firm. His sample thus contained 1687 acquisitions involving a bidder firm listed on the Toronto Stock Exchange, and 413 targets listed on the same exchange.

Eckbo then calculated the "abnormal returns" of the bidder and target firms in his sample for the month of the merger announcement, and for twelve months before and after the merger announcement. The abnormal return is the difference between the realized return on a firm's security and the forecast of the normal or expected return on the security based on market-wide movements in stock prices. If a merger announcement has a significant positive effect on the firm's realized return, then the calculated abnormal return will be positive.

Eckbo found that the 413 target firms on average earned significantly positive abnormal returns as a result of the merger announcement. The average abnormal return over the sample was 3.58 percent in the month of the merger announcement, and 58.2 percent of the sample firms had positive abnormal returns in that month. Eckbo also found that average abnormal returns were positive and significant for the four months leading up to the merger announcement, so that the cumulative average abnormal return for target firms over the announcement month and previous twelve months was 10.02 percent.

With respect to the average abnormal returns of bidder firms, Eckbo found that it was a significant 1.17 percent in the month of the merger announcement, and that 52.1 percent of bidders had positive abnormal returns. The cumulative average abnormal return was 4.31 percent cumulated over the announcement month and the previous 12 months. These results for bidder firms differ from those obtained in U.S. studies in that the bidder firms in U.S. studies typically earn small and insignificant abnormal returns.

38

Eckbo also classified mergers as horizontal and non-horizontal and calculated average abnormal returns for targets and bidders in each group. A merger between two firms was regarded as horizontal if the two firms had one four-digit SIC industry in common. Given that firms with common four-digit SIC industries may not be competing in the same relevant geographic and product market (and therefore might not be able to realize any increase in market power as a result of the merger), it should not come as a surprise that Eckbo's results "do not indicate that firms involved in horizontal mergers perform significantly better than firms in non-horizontal mergers." One cannot conclude from Eckbo's analysis that horizontal mergers in Canada have on average insignificant market power effects. Only a thorough examination of mergers determined to be horizontal on the basis of the application of market definition criteria (see Chapter 4) will allow one to draw conclusions regarding the market power implications of these mergers.[11]

In another study, Eckbo (1988) wished to determine whether or not there were differences in abnormal returns between domestic and foreign bidder firms in Canada. He was particularly interested in exploring whether the creation of Canada's Foreign Investment Review Agency (FIRA) in 1973 had a positive effect on the returns of domestic bidder firms between 1974 and 1984. During these years, FIRA effectively regulated the acquisition of control of Canadian firms by foreign individuals, corporations, governments, or groups containing foreign members. FIRA's powers were reduced at the end of 1984. Eckbo wanted to test whether reduced foreign competition for Canadian target firms (stemming from the higher costs to foreign firms of going through the FIRA application process as well as possible rejection of an application by FIRA) led to an increase in the gains of domestic bidders and a decrease in the gains to domestic targets.

Eckbo found that he could not reject the hypothesis that foreign bidders seeking

---

[11] Baltazar and Santos (2003) carried out an event study of the proposed bank mergers in which they argue that the impact of certain events on the share prices of merger participants and non-participating rival banks can be used to infer the competitive effects of the mergers. In particular, they find that the announcement of the merger between Royal Bank and Bank of Montreal resulted in positive abnormal returns for the merging parties and all but one of the competing banks. This result is consistent, they say, with a merger that is expected to result in increased market power and higher prices. The subsequent announcement of the merger between CIBC and TD Bank resulted in negative abnormal returns for the participating and competing banks. The authors argue that the second merger announcement implied an unacceptable level of concentration that increased the likelihood that both merger proposals would ultimately be rejected. Any gains from merger would therefore be lost.

Chapter 2

Canadian targets on average earned zero economic rents from the acquisition activity whether one looks at the pre-FIRA ten year period 1964-1973, or the post-FIRA ten year period 1974–1983. He also found that domestic bidder firms on average earned a significant 0.8 percent abnormal return in the merger announcement month, and that results for domestic bidder firms between 1964 and 1973 were indistinguishable from the results for domestic bidder firms between 1974 and 1983. He concluded that (1) there was no evidence that FIRA had benefitted domestic bidder firms by reducing competition from foreign firms, (2) there was no evidence that domestic target firms earned larger gains as a result of FIRA's activity, and (3) there was no evidence that FIRA had materially altered the distribution of gains between bidder and target firms in successfully completed acquisitions.

In a more recent study of domestic and foreign acquisitions in Canada using similar data from the 1964 to 1983 period, Eckbo and Thorburn (2000) presented evidence on the performance of Canadian and U.S. bidder firms acquiring Canadian targets. Domestic bidders were found to earn significantly positive announcement period abnormal returns, while U.S. bidder returns were indistinguishable from zero. Eckbo and Thorburn explored several possible explanations for their results. They showed that the smallest Canadian bidders had the greatest average announcement returns. The average U.S. bidder was eight times the size of the average Canadian bidder, so that the insignificant abnormal returns to U.S. bidders may in part be a reflection of the low precision in the abnormal return estimates for relatively large firms. They did not find evidence to support the hypothesis that an attenuation bias due to partial anticipation of a merger helps to explain the poor U.S. bidder performance in Canada. They also suggested that different payment methods for the target firm (e.g. stock versus cash) might help to explain the different returns to domestic U.S. bidder firms.

Event studies of mergers have also been conducted to determine the effects on target firms when the government controls the bidder firm. Eckel and Vermaelen (1986) construct a sample consisting of 14 publicly announced purchases of stock in private or mixed Canadian firms by a provincial government or the federal government, a public corporation, or a mixed enterprise between July 1973 and January 1982. The 14 target firms were broken down into two sub-samples containing seven unregulated firms and seven regulated firms. In the week of the merger announcement, the unregulated target firms experienced a significant negative average abnormal return of –9.3 percent, while the regulated target firms experienced a significant positive average abnormal return of 10.5 percent. The regulated firm's cumulative average abnormal return remained stable

40

in the four weeks after the merger announcement, while the unregulated firms experienced a reduction of 10 percent in cumulative average abnormal returns. Eckel and Vermaelen suggested that the negative returns for unregulated target firms could be due to an increase in agency costs once the government took over a private or mixed firm, whereas agency costs were not expected to increase significantly for regulated companies because of the agency costs of existing regulation. They further suggested (at page 400) that "internal regulation through direct ownership may be less costly than external regulation and may also benefit shareholders through increased access to low-visibility subsidiaries."

IV. ECONOMIES OF SCALE AND RETURNS TO SCALE

An important characteristic of market structure is the extent to which firms in a market can exploit economies of scale in production. Carlton and Perloff (2004, Ch. 2) discuss reasons for economies of scale and some of the empirical studies that have attempted to measure scale economies. Here the focus is on studies of scale economies and returns to scale in a Canadian context.

In 1978, the Royal Commission on Corporate Concentration released a report that contained a survey of the studies of scale economies that had been made for Canadian industries. The results of Eastman and Stykolt's (1967) classic study were cited. Using the engineering approach, they found that in about one-third of their sample of 16 industries, no plants were of minimum efficient scale (MES); in a second third, less than 60 percent of industry capacity was of efficient scale, while in only one industry was all industry capacity at MES. Eastman and Stykolt concluded that a significant percentage of Canadian production came from plants of inefficient scale.

The Commission wrote that similar results were obtained by Gorecki (1976) in his empirical analysis of scale economies. Gorecki reported that based on engineering studies of Pratten (1971) and Scherer (1973), the number of MES plants compatible with Canadian consumption in 1968 was, for a sample of 17 industries, always much smaller than the actual number of plants. This result would be somewhat modified by Gorecki's own survivor estimates of MES plant size since these were substantially smaller than the engineering estimates.

Still, on the basis of its review of the evidence, the Royal Commission on Corporate

Concentration (1978, p. 67) concluded that "Plant-specific economies of scale...are significant in a few Canadian industries but have not, in general, imposed a major cost disadvantage on Canadian firms in serving the Canadian market." Rather two "more important" sources of scale inefficiency in Canada were identified. First, Canadian firms in tariff-protected industries produced a more diverse line of products in a plant than did U.S. firms in the same industries, Canadian plants employed less specialized equipment, had a higher proportion of set-up and downtime, and experienced fewer scale economies arising from learning by doing. Second, Canadian firms were found to have a relatively low level of research and development because of the degree of foreign ownership of Canadian firms, the small size of firms, and the high product diversity within firms. [12] The issue of product diversity within plants will be further addressed below.

Fuss and Gupta (1981) produced estimates of MES, returns to scale and suboptimal capacity for 91 four-digit Canadian manufacturing industries using statistical cost analysis. Their procedure involved assuming a homothetic production function and cost-minimizing behaviour, so that the relevant scale curve information is contained in the relationship between average variable cost and output. Capital data are unnecessary for the estimation of the scale curve under their assumptions because it may be estimated from data on operating costs alone. Their procedure also allowed them to conduct their estimation of the scale curve using pooled cross section and time series data. They had data on seven size-groups of plants for 91 industries for the years 1965, 1968, 1969 and 1970, and so they had 28 observations per industry.

Table 2.3 summarizes the characteristics of the scale curves that they have estimated. Note that 73 of the 91 industries have an MES that is 5 percent or less of industry output and that the cost disadvantage at one-half MES output is five percent or less for 82 of the 91 industries. Also consistent with earlier results, Fuss and Gupta found a large proportion of their industries characterized by suboptimal capacity (e.g., 69 industries have suboptimal capacity between 11 and 100 percent).

Table 2.4 presents a comparison of engineering estimates of MES reported in Gorecki (1976) and the cost function estimates of Fuss and Gupta for 11 comparable industries. The cost disadvantage ratio (or penalty for production at below MES) is also reported for

---

[12] This discussion has been based on material in the *Report of the Royal Commission on Corporate Concentration* (1978), pp. 52–55, 67, adapted and reproduced with the permission of the Minister of Public Works and Government Services Canada, 2004, and courtesy of the Privy Council Office.

Table 2.3
Summary of Characteristics of Scale Curves Estimated by Fuss and Gupta (1981)

(a) *Shape of scale curve*

	U-Shaped	L-Shaped	Hyperbolic declining	Straight line declining
No. of industries	26	29	5	31

(b) *MES as percentage of industry output*

	0–2%	2.1–5.0%	5.1–10.0%	10.1–20.0%	20.1–100%
No. of industries	52	21	14	4	0

(c) *Extent of cost disadvantage at one-half MES*

	0.1–1.0%	1.1–2.0%	2.1–5.0%	5.1–10.0%	>10.0%
No. of industries	18	26	38	6	3

(d) *Percentage of suboptimal capacity*

	0–10.9%	11.0–30.9%	31.0–50.9%	51–100%
No. of industries	22	25	25	19

these industries. The cost function estimates of MES are smaller than the engineering estimates for the same reason that survivor estimates are smaller than engineering estimates: they are based on actually observed plant sizes. Fuss and Gupta concluded that sample-based estimates of MES like the cost function estimates probably underestimate true MES, while the engineering estimates may be overestimates. However, assuming that engineering estimates are the best estimates of actual MES, Fuss and Gupta concluded that their cost function estimates of MES could also serve as good proxies for actual MES because they were highly correlated with the engineering estimates (while the survivor estimates were not).

Table 2.4
Engineering and Cost Function Estimates of MES and the Slope of Long Run Average Cost

Industry	MES as a Percentage of Industry Size		Estimates of the Slope of Long Run Average Cost	
	Engineering Estimates (1967)	Cost Function Estimates (1968)	Engineering Estimates at MES/3	Cost Function Estimates at MES/2
Bakeries	2.5	0.84	b	c
Breweries	34.5	8.85	5.0	4.80
Cigarettes	76.9	13.13	2.2	2.35
Non-rubber shoes	1.7	0.07	1.5	0.01
Steel	38.5	7.34	11.0	1.62
Storage batteries	21.7	3.32	4.6	2.46
Cement	15.2	4.19	26.0	36.60
Glass bottles	13.9	6.84	11.0	4.53
Petroleum refining	16.7	1.09	4.8	1.65
Paint and varnish	15.9	1.95	4.4	5.04
Soap	20.8	4.37	b	c

[a] The slope of long run average cost is measured by the percentage by which average cost increases by moving to one-half or one-third of MES. [b] Unavailable. [c] Not computed.

Source: Table 2 in Fuss and Gupta (1981). The engineering estimates of MES are from Gorecki (1976, 48). His sources are Scherer et al. (1975, p. 94) for the second to tenth industries and Pratten (1971) for the first and eleventh industries. The engineering estimates of the slope of the long run average cost curve are from Scherer et al. (1975, p. 80). The cost function estimates of MES and the slope of the long run average cost curve are from Fuss and Gupta (1981, p. 133).

Baldwin and Gorecki (1986a) have produced further estimates of returns to scale for a sample of Canadian industries. They obtained their estimates from the direct estimation of a Cobb-Douglas production function using ordinary least squares. Using data on two-digit manufacturing industries, they found that across the manufacturing sector as a whole, in both 1970 and 1979, Canadian industry experienced increasing returns to scale and the incidence of returns to scale was similar in both years (1.155 and 1.153 in 1970 and 1979, respectively). In both 1970 and 1979, 16 of the two-digit industries exhibited increasing returns to scale, while four exhibited constant returns to scale. They found that Fuss and Gupta's cost-based scale elasticity estimates were generally lower than their own. Fuss and Gupta's estimates showed increasing returns to scale, but they were generally not significantly different from one and averaged only 1.03, compared to Baldwin and Gorecki's average scale elasticity of 1.17 using the production function.[13]

Robidoux and Lester (1992) have produced more recent estimates of economies of scale by using observations on 147 Canadian manufacturing industries in 1979. A variation on Fuss and Gupta's (1981) methodology was employed. The authors concluded that the majority of manufacturing industries exhibited increasing returns to scale, and only a small number exhibited decreasing returns to scale. Suboptimal scale was estimated to result in a cost penalty of approximately four percent of total manufacturing costs. The authors estimated the average scale elasticity to be 1.06, closer to Fuss and Gupta's (1981) than to Baldwin and Gorecki's (1986a) estimate.

Finally, Benarroch (1997) considered whether returns to scale in Canadian manufacturing were national in nature, regional, or internal to the industry. The author used data for manufacturing industries (at the two-digit SIC level) for the period 1961–1990. Benarroch (1997, p. 1084) found that "at the two-digit SIC level there are increasing returns to scale in Canadian manufacturing industries that are national in nature and external to both the industry and the province." This was taken to indicate the presence of "beneficial spillovers that occur across industries and provinces in Canada; productivity growth in individual industries or provinces benefits from the expansion of manufacturing as a whole."

V. SCALE AND SPECIALIZATION

In the past, it was frequently suggested that Canadian plants were small relative to their U.S. counterparts, that they produced too many products with short production runs, and that these characteristics of Canadian production stemmed from the relatively small size

---

[13] Baldwin and Gorecki (1986a) obtained similar results in their analysis of 167 four-digit Canadian manufacturing industries. In particular, in 1970 and 1979, 78 and 64 percent, respectively, of value added of the Canadian manufacturing sector were found in industries characterized by increasing returns to scale. There were only three industries with decreasing returns to scale in 1970 and 1979, while 20 percent and 32 percent of sector value added in 1970 and 1979, respectively, were found in industries with constant returns to scale.

of the Canadian market and the tariff which affected the competition faced by Canadian producers. Baldwin and Gorecki addressed these issues in a series of papers, and McFetridge (1986) and Baldwin and Gorecki (1986b) summarized the results of their investigations.

First, comparing the larger plants (those accounting for the top 50 percent of industry employment) in the U.S. and Canada in 125 matched Canadian and U.S. industries, Baldwin and Gorecki (1986b) found that a substantial scale disadvantage for Canada was evident. The weighted average ratio of Canadian to U.S. plant size was 0.762 in 1970 and 0.818 in 1979.

Second, using data from 119 Canadian four-digit SIC manufacturing industries for the years 1974 and 1979, Baldwin and Gorecki (1986b) found that product diversity in Canadian manufacturing industries was reduced slightly, but the size of an average plant increased substantially. The net effect was an increase in the average production run by 55 percent. Using a regression analysis, they found that plants became larger both by producing more products and by increasing the length of the production run. However, the rate at which the first occurred declined with size, implying that plant scale economies that would lead to greater diversity were eventually exhausted. In a number of industries they found that length of production run continued to increase across the entire plant size range (even though the length of production run increased at a decreasing rate with increasing plant size).

Third, Baldwin and Gorecki (1986b) found that increases in market size and concentration across their sample of industries led to significant increases in the size of Canadian plants relative to the size of U.S. plants. In industries with high ownership concentration and high tariffs, only decreases in effective tariff protection significantly increased the size of Canadian plants relative to their U.S. counterparts.[14]

Fourth, with respect to the average length of the production run in 1970 and 1979, Baldwin and Gorecki (1983) found that an industry's average production run was longer the greater the average plant size, the smaller the number of products coded to the

---

[14] See Baldwin and Gorecki (1986b) in D.G. McFetridge, ed., *Canadian Industry in Transition*, pp. 214–223, adapted and reproduced with the permission of the Minister of Public Works and Government Services Canada, 2004, and courtesy of the Privy Council Office.

industry, and the greater the number of plants per firm. Furthermore, the average length of production run associated with a given average plant size was shorter in high-tariff and high-concentration industries.

According to McFetridge (1986),

> The authors interpret their results as support for the view proposed by Eastman and Stykolt (1967) that high-tariff, high concentration industries are characterized by sub-optimal plant scales and excessive product diversity. The view that the effect of high tariffs and high concentration is exacerbated by foreign ownership is not supported by their results. Their results also imply that the tariff reductions which occurred in the 1970s were salutary in that they increased the relative scale of plants in high-tariff, high-concentration industries and increased run lengths, proportional to scale, in all industries.[15]

VI. ENTRY AND EXIT

Another characteristic of Canadian market structure that has received some attention from economists is the extent of entry and exit in different industries. These studies have focused for the most part on data for the 1970s and 1980s, and there appears to be a lack of entry and exit data for more recent years. Baldwin and Gorecki's (1991b) study of entry and exit in the Canadian manufacturing sector was motivated by a concern that economists were underestimating the importance of entry because they rarely had the opportunity to measure on a broad basis the cumulative effects of entry. Baldwin and Gorecki used establishment-based data extending from 1970 to the early 1980s that were from the Canadian Census of Manufacturers. Plants and firms have been assigned identifiers by the Census that allow them to be tracked over time, and permit entry, exit and continuing plant activity to be calculated. Some of their important results for entry into and exit from the manufacturing sector as a whole can be summarized as follows:

---

[15] McFetridge (1986, p. 39) goes on to write that "Predictions regarding the impact of future trade liberalization depend on which of these results one uses, on the nature of the trade liberalization envisaged, and on the weight, if any, attached to statistically insignificant regression coefficients." A further caution is urged in the interpretation of their results because of the joint dependence of many of Baldwin and Gorecki's independent variables.

(a)   On average, from 1970 to 1982, new firms that were created every year accounted for 4.9 percent of the total number of firms in the manufacturing sector. Also on average from 1970 to 1982, 6.5 percent of existing firms exited every year. Greenfield entry by opening a new plant accounted for 4.3 percent of the total number of firms, while entry by acquisition accounted for only 0.6 percent of firms. The number of exits that were the result of closedowns, 5.3 percent of existing firms, was larger than the number of exits that occurred by divestiture, 1.2 percent of existing firms.

(b)   Greenfield entrants had a high mortality rate soon after entry. They tended to fail at higher rates than do older firms, but a significant percentage were still in operation ten years after entry. For example, of the 1,427 greenfield entrants in 1971, while 10.6 percent exited within the first year, 40.2 percent were still operating in 1982.

(c)   Close-down exits in a given year were not confined to recent entrants. For example, in 1970–71, 18.3 percent of exits by plant closure were by firms that entered that year, while 81.7 percent of the exits were by firms that existed at the beginning of the year.

(d)   The average percentage of all firms accounted for by each entry cohort declined continuously from 1971 to 1980, while the average value-added share increased. The growth rate of surviving entrants more than offset the effects of early exit by each cohort of entrants.

(e)   The significance of entry and exit is even more apparent when cumulated over periods of six to eleven years. For example, from 1970 to 1981, 44 percent of the 1970 population of firms had exited the manufacturing sector by 1981 either by plant closing or divestiture. From 1970 to 1981, the number of entrants by either plant openings or acquisitions equalled 40 percent of the 1970 firm population.

Baldwin and Gorecki (1991b) also examined entry into and exit from 167 four-digit Canadian manufacturing industries between 1970 and 1979, and the results are reported in Table 2.5 (which reproduces their Table 4). Entry and exit calculations were made in terms of the proportion of number of establishments involved as well as the proportion of shares of industry shipments. The proportions reported in the table are the means across the 167 industries. The results using this data are consistent with the results for

Table 2.5
Average Share of Number of Establishments and Average Share of Shipments Across 167 Four-Digit Canadian Manufacturing Industries for Various Categories of Entry and Exit, 1970 and 1979

		Share of Number of Establishments[a]		Share of Shipments[a]	
	Firm category	**1970**	**1979**	**1970**	**1979**
1.	All firms[b]	100.0	100.0	100.0	100.0
2.	All entrants[c]		33.2		26.8
i.	By plant birth		18.8		11.5
ii.	By acquisition		8.7		10.7
iii.	By plant switch		5.6		4.6
3.	All exits[d]	39.8		30.9	
i.	By plant closing	24.6		13.3	
ii.	By divestiture	10.0		12.7	
iii.	By plant switch	5.2		4.9	
4.	All continuing firms[e]	60.2	66.8	69.1	73.2
i.	Continuing plants[f]	55.3	59.2	63.4	65.0
ii.	Divested	0.6		1.1	
iii.	Acquired		2.2		3.0
iv.	Plant closures	3.8		3.8	
v.	Plant births		4.6		4.4
vi.	Plant switches	0.5	0.7	0.8	0.9

[a] The average is calculated across all 167 observations. [b] The sample consists of a reduced set of plants that report extensive information to the Canadian Census of Manufactures. [c] Firms that entered a four-digit industry between 1970 and 1979 by plant birth, acquisition, or by switching a plant from another industry. [d] Firms that exited an industry between 1970 and 1979 by closing a plant, divesting themselves of plant, or switching plant to another industry. [e] Firms that existed in both 1970 and 1979. [f] Continuing plants are those that existed in the four-digit industry in both 1970 and 1979 and did not undergo a change in ownership.

Source: Table 4 in Baldwin and Gorecki (1991b).

entry into and exit from manufacturing as a whole. As of 1979, new entrants since 1970 accounted for, on average, 33 percent of all establishments and 27 percent of all shipments. Firm exits from 1970 to 1979 accounted for, on average, 40 percent of the number of establishments in 1970 and 31 percent of shipments. Note that the most important form of entry is by opening a new plant, while the most important form of exit is by closing a plant (although the relative importance of plant opening and plant closing varies depending on whether number of establishments or shipments is used to measure entry and exit).

Baldwin and Gorecki (1991b) concluded that their results were consistent with a number of results obtained in other studies (to the extent that meaningful comparisons are possible given differences in the definitions of entry and exit, differences in time periods, and different data bases). Baldwin and Gorecki (1991a) also suggested that their mobility statistics helped to correct the misleading impression conveyed by slowly changing concentration ratios that Canadian industrial market structures are characterized by stability in their firm populations.

There have been few Canadian studies of the determinants of entry and exit. One study of the entry process in Canadian manufacturing by Baldwin and Gorecki (1987) used data from 141 four-digit Canadian manufacturing industries from 1970 to 1979. The authors examined entry by plant creation versus diversified merger, and entry by domestic as opposed to foreign firms. Baldwin and Gorecki found that there was generally less new plant creation in industries with higher entry barriers, but more entry via merger. They found (a) domestic firms responded to profitability, while foreign firms did not, (b) domestic firms responded to export growth, while foreign firms did not, and (c) domestic firms were not affected by entry barriers, while foreign firm diversified entry was stimulated by entry barriers.

Recent Canadian studies of the causes of success and failure of entrants have used survey techniques. Johnson et al. (1997) used a survey of 4000 firms (with a response rate of 80 percent) to study the causes of success of new entrants. The authors considered many factors, including management strategy and financial practices. While a complete discussion of their results is not practical here, one important conclusion is that innovation is a strong contributor to the growth of entrants. In another study, Baldwin et al. (1997) used results of a survey of corporate bankruptcies in Canada conducted during March 1 to August 31, 1996 to study the causes of exit through bankruptcy. Bankruptcy trustees for 550 firms answered questionnaires. Baldwin et al. concluded that both external shocks (such as economic downturns) and internal deficiencies of the firms contributed to bankruptcy. Inexperienced management and poor financial planning were found to be important causes of bankruptcy.

Strategic barriers to entry may be important in Canadian markets containing either a dominant firm or a small number of firms. West (1981) has found some evidence to support the hypothesis that a supermarket firm used preemptive behaviour to deter entry into its market, while West and Von Hohenbalken (1984) and Von Hohenbalken and West (1984) found evidence consistent with a supermarket firm engaging in spatial predation to deter entry (see Chapter 4 for a more detailed discussion). The latter studies of strategic entry barriers focussed on one market and one industry. Success at detecting strategic entry deterrence is likely to be greater using the market/industry study approach since entry deterring strategies can be complex, and may be discernible only after a detailed time series analysis of market specific entry and exit data.

VII. MARKET STRUCTURE AND INDUSTRIAL PERFORMANCE

During the 1960s, 1970s and 1980s, economists produced a number of studies that attempted to explain industrial performance, measured by profits or prices, with variables measuring different characteristics of market structure. Carlton and Perloff (2004, Chapter 8) provide a theoretical analysis of several measures of performance used in these studies, as well as some of the variables measuring market structure, and they summarize some of the empirical results relating structure to performance based on U.S. data. In this section, some of the more prominent Canadian studies of market structure and industrial performance will be reviewed. In addition, we consider modern studies of market structure, conduct and performance in the Canadian airline, gasoline and banking industries.

Structure-Conduct-Performance Studies

McFetridge (1973) examined the relationship between market structure and price-cost margins using cross-section data on 43 three-digit Canadian manufacturing industries for the period 1965–1969. Market structure variables included those designed to measure the rate of growth of demand, the number and size distribution of sellers, the regional dispersion of production, whether the industry is a producer or consumer goods industry, economies of scale, advertising intensity, capital intensity, and effective tariff protection.

McFetridge found that a variety of measures of industry concentration were significant in explaining price-cost margins. It was found that the effect of an increase in concentration was greater when the level of concentration was greater, and that concentration had a greater effect on price-cost margins in consumer goods than in producer goods industries. The study offered no strong findings regarding entry barriers or other variables.

Jones, Laudadio and Percy (1973) examined the relationship between the profit rate and market structure using cross-section data on 30 three-digit consumer goods industries for 1965. Market structure variables included those designed to measure concentration, the rate of growth in demand, barriers to entry, whether the industry operated in regional markets, and foreign competition. The authors concluded that increased concentration increased the profit rate, as did increased barriers to entry (in particular the advertising-to-sales ratio) and increased demand growth. In addition, the authors found that increased foreign competition increased industry profits. The authors argued that this could be in part due to a correspondence between high imports and high demand.

Several other structure-performance studies also have attempted to explore the impact of Canada's tariff on prices and profits in Canadian manufacturing industries. Bloch (1974) examined the influence of concentration and tariffs on prices and costs using a sample of twenty corresponding Canadian and U.S. manufacturing industries and data from 1963 or 1965. He found (p. 602) that "high Canadian tariffs and levels of concentration have an upward influence on Canadian prices relative to the prices of foreign competitors in import-competing industries. The influence of tariffs and concentration on relative prices are strictly interdependent. Neither high tariffs nor high concentration is associated with significantly higher relative prices in the absence of the other." He also found that concentration influenced profitability, while tariffs did not.

Similar results are presented by Hazledine (1980), who studied cross-section data on relative Canadian/U.S. prices and costs, tariff protection and market structure characteristics for 33 manufactured commodities. Hazledine tested the law-of-one-price model, which predicts that the domestic price of a good will be equal to its world price plus the value of protection from tariffs and transport costs, and the market-power model, which focuses on domestic market structure and costs as determinants of price. Hazledine (p. 152) found that "(1) tariff protection does matter, but only in association with seller concentration, (2) relative costs are most important in unconcentrated industries, (3) the market power model is statistically better supported than the law-of-one-price."

Caves et al. (1980) estimated structure performance models using alternative measures of profits and using data on 84 Canadian manufacturing industries for 1968. The authors found that imports acted like a competitive fringe in limiting the market power of concentrated industries. The measure of scale economies had no power to explain profits in Canadian manufacturing industries. The authors found some support for the hypothesis that profits will be lower when oligopolistic tacit coordination is more difficult, and some indication that profits were lower in sectors where buyers might have had market power. There was weak support for the hypothesis that profits are reduced by union bargaining power. As well, the authors found that profits of foreign subsidiaries and the profits of Canadian companies were not determined by the same influence, and that the subsidiaries' measured profits may poorly reflect their actual profits.

Finally, Baldwin and Gorecki (1985) examined determinants of small plant market share in Canadian manufacturing industries in the 1970s. For each industry, they considered the proportion of the industry's sales accounted for by plants below MES. They found that their measure of suboptimal plant size was larger in high tariff/high concentration industries, but that this was offset as market size increased for such industries. Baldwin and Gorecki's results are thus consistent with those of Eastman and Stykolt (1967), Bloch (1974) and Caves et al. (1980).

Studies relating market structure variables to industrial performance have come under a great deal of criticism, which likely explains the lack of such studies since the mid-1980s. Criticisms of these studies are summarized in Carlton and Perloff (2004, Chapter 8), and include both concerns about the measurement of the variables used, and conceptual concerns. Measurement concerns include difficulties in measuring marginal costs and economic profits and the fact that data are often available only aggregated to the industry level, which may include many separate markets. One conceptual concern is that these studies typically assume that the same relationship between structure and performance holds across all industries. As well, these studies ignore the fact that while market structure may cause performance, firm conduct and performance may also affect market structure.

For these reasons, recent studies of market power, performance or conduct have focused on particular markets or industries, using data on a single market over time or on multiple markets within an industry. As well, many recent studies avoid measurement problems by not using accounting data on costs, and solve interpretive problems by estimating models derived directly from economic theory. In the remainder of this section, we summarize recent results for three Canadian industries: airline, banking, and retail gasoline industries.

Airlines

While there have been a number of published studies of market structure, conduct, and market power for the U.S. airline industry, no similar studies exist for Canada. This is somewhat surprising given the high level of concentration in the industry reported by the Competition Bureau and given the recent merger of Air Canada and Canadian Airlines.

Banks

Several studies within the last fifteen years have estimated the degree of market power being exercised in banking, or the relationship between market structure, conduct, and performance in the banking industry. Shaffer (1993) used annual time series data on interest rates, assets, input prices, and the interest rates on government T-bills for the period 1965 to 1989. Shaffer estimated a demand function and a behavioural equation for the banking sector, which provided an estimate of the degree of market power being exercised. He concluded that the annual aggregate data were consistent with perfect competition, and strongly reject perfect collusion at monopoly levels.

Other studies, however, have reached different conclusions using different methods and data. Heffernan (1994) used data from 1987 to 1990 to estimate the relationship between firm specific interest rates on various products and government bond rates and the number of competing firms offering the same product and term (along with other control variables). Heffernan found that for most specifications and product categories, interest rates did depend upon the number of competing firms. This result was interpreted as supporting Cournot-type behaviour. In contrast with previous Canadian studies, Mallet and Sen (2001) estimated the relationship between interest rates set by financial institutions for small business loans and the number of competing lenders within a local geographic area. The authors found that an increase in the number of local competitors lowered the interest rates charged on small-business loans, again in contrast with Shaffer's conclusion of perfect competition.

Gasoline

There have been few attempts to estimate the degree of market power being exploited in Canadian retail gasoline markets. Slade (1986, 1987) considered retail pricing of gasoline in the Vancouver, B.C. area during a price war which took place in the summer of 1983. Slade concluded that while noncooperative Nash equilibrium behaviour can be rejected, the observed prices were less than what a monopolist would set.

Other studies have used panel data for large Canadian cities to consider whether price levels and volatility are related to concentration and the presence of retailers that do not sell refinery-brand gasoline (known as "independents"). Sen (2003) studied citywide average monthly retail gasoline prices for major Canadian cities from 1991 to 1997, and found that although higher local concentration (on the city level) was associated with higher retail prices, wholesale prices explained more of the variation in retail prices than did market concentration. Eckert (2003) and Noel (2003) demonstrated that lower average retail prices and higher price volatility were related to lower concentration and the presence of independents. Eckert and West (2004) found, however, that the effect of independents on retail prices was greatest on stations within close proximity to independents and that the effect weakened as independents were located farther away. In general, therefore, there appears to be strong evidence that concentration and the presence of independents are significant determinants of retail prices in Canadian gasoline markets.

VIII. SUMMARY

This chapter has presented some of the empirical evidence on a number of aspects of Canadian market structure. Concentration in Canadian industry was examined first, and it was found that the level of industrial concentration varies significantly by industry. While there is some evidence that the level of industrial concentration has been relatively stable, it can change quite rapidly if large-scale mergers in an industry are approved. Such mergers occurred in the Canadian petroleum industry in 1989, the airline industry in 1999, and were attempted in the banking industry in 1998.

Given the impact that merger activity can have on market structure, merger activity in Canada was reviewed next, and special attention was given to the valuation effects of corporate acquisitions in Canada that are derived in event studies of mergers. It has been found that both bidder firms and target firms have on average benefited from mergers, but the gains to the targets have exceeded those to the bidders.

Studies that have estimated scale economies in Canadian manufacturing industry were then surveyed, and differences between survivor, engineering and cost function estimates were discussed. This was followed by a summary of some recent results on scale and specialization in Canadian manufacturing industry. There is some evidence that Canadian plants have historically been small relative to their U.S. counterparts, and that they have produced too many products with short production runs. These characteristics of Canadian production were partly attributed to the relatively small size of the Canadian market and the tariff that affected the competition faced by Canadian producers.

Recent calculations of the extent of entry into and exit from Canadian manufacturing industry are reported next. The mobility statistics show that contrary to the impression of stable market structure conveyed by concentration statistics, Canadian industrial structure has undergone many internal changes over time. Studies that have examined the determinants of entry and exit, and the causes of success and failure of entrants are also briefly discussed.

Finally, a survey was made of some of the more prominent studies of Canadian market structure and industrial performance. Market structure and performance studies, as well as other studies estimating the degree of market power being exercised, carried out for banking and retail gasoline industries are also discussed.

REFERENCES

Baldwin, John R. and Paul K. Gorecki. 1983. "Trade, Tariffs, Product Diversity and Length of Production Run in Canadian Manufacturing Industries: 1970–79," Discussion Paper No. 247, Economic Council of Canada.

Baldwin, John R. and Paul K. Gorecki. 1985. "The Determinants of Small Plant Market Share in Canadian Manufacturing Industries in the 1970s," *Review of Economics and Statistics* 67: 156–161.

Baldwin, John R. and Paul K. Gorecki. 1986a. *The Role of Scale in Canada–U.S. Productivity Differences*. Toronto: University of Toronto Press.

Baldwin, John R. and Paul K. Gorecki. 1986b. "Canada–U.S. Productivity Differences in the Manufacturing Sector: 1970–1979," in Donald G. McFetridge, ed., *Canadian Industry in Transition*. Toronto: University of Toronto Press.

Baldwin, John R. and Paul K. Gorecki. 1987. "Plant Creation Versus Plant Acquisition: The Entry Process in Canadian Manufacturing," *International Journal of Industrial Organization* 5: 27–41.

Baldwin, John R. and Paul K. Gorecki. 1991a. "Firm Turnover and Market Structure: Concentration Statistics as a Misleading Practice," in R.S. Khemani and W.T. Stanbury, eds., *Canadian Competition Law and Policy at the Centenary*. Halifax: Institute for Research on Public Policy.

Baldwin, John R. and Paul K. Gorecki. 1991b. "Firm Entry and Exit in the Canadian Manufacturing Sector, 1970–1982," *Canadian Journal of Economics* 24: 300–323.

Baldwin, John R., Tara Gray, Joanne Johnson, Jody Proctor, Mohammed Rafiquzzaman, and David Sabourin. 1997. *Failing Concerns: Business Bankruptcy in Canada*. Statistics Canada Catalogue No. 61–525–XIE. Ottawa: Minister of Industry.

Baltazar, Ramon and Michael Santos. 2003. "The Benefits of Banking Mega–Mergers: Event Study Evidence from the 1998 Failed Mega–Merger Attempts in Canada," *Canadian Journal of Administrative Sciences* 20: 196–208.

Benarroch, Michael. 1997. "Returns to scale in Canadian Manufacturing: An Interprovincial Comparison," *Canadian Journal of Economics* 30: 1083–1103.

Bloch, Harry. 1974. "Prices, Costs, and Profits in Canadian Manufacturing: The Influence of Tariffs and Concentration," *Canadian Journal of Economics* 7: 594–610.

Carlton, Dennis W. and Jeffrey M. Perloff. 2004. *Modern Industrial Organization*, Fourth Edition. New York: Pearson Education.

Caves, Richard E., Michael E. Porter, A. Michael Spence, and John T. Scott. 1980.

Competition in the Open Economy: A Model Applied to Canada. Cambridge: Harvard University Press.

Eastman, H.C. and S. Stykolt. 1967. *The Tariff and Competition in Canada*. Toronto: Macmillan.

Eckbo, B. Espen. 1986. "Mergers and the Market for Corporate Control: The Canadian Evidence," *Canadian Journal of Economics* 19: 236–260.

Eckbo, B. Espen. 1988. "The Market for Corporate Control: Policy Issues and Capital Market Evidence," in R.S. Khemani, D.M. Shapiro, and W.T. Stanbury, eds., *Mergers, Corporate Concentration and Power in Canada*. Halifax: Institute for Research on Public Policy.

Eckbo, B. Espen and Karin S. Thorburn. 2000. "Gains to Bidder Firms Revisited: Domestic and Foreign Acquisitions in Canada," *Journal of Financial and Quantitative Analysis* 35: 1–25.

Eckel, Catherine and Theo Vermaelen. 1986. "Internal Regulation: The Effects of Government Ownership on the Value of the Firm," *Journal of Law and Economics* 29: 381–403.

Eckert, Andrew. 2003. "Retail Price Cycles and the Presence of Small Firms," *International Journal of Industrial Organization* 21: 151–170.

Eckert, Andrew and Douglas S. West. 2004. "Retail Gasoline Price Cycles across Spatially Dispersed Gasoline Stations," *Journal of Law and Economics,* forthcoming.

Fuss, Melvyn A. and Vinod K. Gupta. 1981. "A Cost Function Approach to the Estimation of Minimum Efficient Scale, Returns to Scale, and Suboptimal Capacity," *European Economic Review* 15: 123–135. Reprinted with permission from Elsevier.

Gorecki, Paul K. 1976. *Economies of Scale and Efficient Plant Size in Canadian Manufacturing Industries*, Research Monograph No. 1, Bureau of Competition Policy, Consumer and Corporate Affairs. Ottawa: Minister of Supply and Services Canada.

Hazledine, Tim. 1980. "Testing Two Models of Pricing and Protection with Canada/ United States Data," *Journal of Industrial Economics* 29: 145–155.

Heffernan, Shelagh. 1994. "Competition in the Canadian Personal Finance Sector," *International Journal of the Economics of Business* 1: 323–342.

Johnson, Joanne, John Baldwin, and Christine Hinchley. 1997. Successful Entrants: Creating the Capacity for Survival and Growth. Statistics Canada Catalogue No. 61-525-XPE. Ottawa: Minister of Industry.

Jones, J.C.H., L. Laudadio, and M. Percy. 1973. "Market Structure and Profitability in Canadian Manufacturing Industry: Some Cross-Section Results," *Canadian Journal of Economics* 6: 356–368.

Mallet, Ted and Anindya Sen. 2001. "Does Local Competition Impact Interest Rates Charged on Small Business Loans? Empirical Evidence from Canada," *Review of Industrial Organization* 19: 437–452.

McFetridge, Donald G. 1973. "Market Structure and Price–Cost Margins: An Analysis of the Canadian Manufacturing Sector," *Canadian Journal of Economics* 6: 344–355.

McFetridge, Donald G. 1986. "The Economics of Industrial Structure: An Overview," in Donald G. McFetridge, ed., *Canadian Industry in Transition*. Toronto: University of Toronto Press.

Noel, Michael. 2003. "Edgeworth Price Cycles, Cost–based Pricing and Sticky Pricing in Retail Gasoline Markets," Univ. of California at San Diego Working Paper.

Pratten, C.F. 1971. *Economies of Scale in Manufacturing Industry*. Cambridge: Cambridge University Press.

Robidoux, Benoit and John Lester. 1992. "Econometric Estimates of Scale Economies in Canadian Manufacturing," *Applied Economics* 24: 113–122.

Royal Commission on Corporate Concentration. 1978. *Report of the Royal Commission on Corporate Concentration*. Ottawa: Minister of Supply and Services Canada.

Scherer, F.M. 1973. "The Determinants of Industrial Plant Sizes in Six Nations," *Review of Economics and Statistics* 55: 135–145.

Scherer, F.M., Alan Beckenstein, Erich Kaufer, and R. Dennis Murphy. 1975. *The Economics of Multi–Plant Operation*. Cambridge: Harvard University Press.

Sen, Anindya. 2003. "Higher Prices at Canadian Gas Pumps: International Crude Oil Prices or Local Market Concentration? An Empirical Investigation," *Energy Economics* 25: 269–288.

Shaffer, Sherrill. 1993. "A Test of Competition in Canadian Banking," *Journal of Money, Credit, and Banking* 25: 49–61.

Slade, Margaret. 1987. "Interfirm Rivalry in a Repeated Game: An Empirical Test of Tacit Collusion," *Journal of Industrial Economics* 35: 499–516.

Slade, Margaret. 1986. "Conjectures, Firm Characteristics, and Market Structure: An Empirical Assessment," *International Journal of Industrial Organization* 4: 347–369.

Von Hohenbalken, Balder and Douglas S. West. 1984. "Predation among Supermarkets: An Algorithmic Locational Analysis," *Journal of Urban Economics* 15: 244–257.

West, Douglas S. 1981. "Testing for Market Preemption Using Sequential Location Data," *Bell Journal of Economics* 12: 129–143.

West, Douglas S. and Balder Von Hohenbalken. 1984. "Spatial Predation in a Canadian Retail Oligopoly," *Journal of Regional Science* 24: 415–429.

CHAPTER 3

PATENTS AND RESEARCH AND DEVELOPMENT

I. INTRODUCTION

Over the years, a number of issues have been raised regarding Canada's ability to compete in the global economy. Some of the issues arose from concerns that the level of research and development in Canada was too low, that there was too heavy a reliance on imported technology, and that too few patents were being obtained by Canadian firms. In this chapter, some empirical evidence will be presented to address these issues, beginning with some figures on patents, and followed by a discussion of research and development in Canada. The chapter concludes by examining the contentious issue of compulsory licensing in the Canadian pharmaceutical industry, and reviews some of the findings on how changes in Canada's patent policy have affected pharmaceutical prices and research and development.

II. PATENTS

A brief history, discussion, and analysis of Canada's patent system as it had evolved to 1970 is contained in the Economic Council of Canada's (1971) *Report on Intellectual and Industrial Property*.[1] According to that document, Canada's patent system originated in 1823, when Lower Canada introduced an act based on the British Statute of Monopolies of 1624. Following Confederation, the *Patent Act* of 1869 superseded this act and similar acts passed by other provinces. One of the features of this act was a provision that stated that a patent would be revoked if the patentee did not manufacture its invention in Canada within three years (reduced to two years in 1872). A new *Patent Act* was passed in 1923 and it contained some new provisions relating to patents on food and medicine. The next major revision to the *Patent Act* came in 1935. It contained a list of six potential patent abuses which, if proven, could permit the revocation of a patent or the grant of compulsory licenses to persons who wished to use the patented invention. The *Patent Act* has been amended from time to time since 1935. According to Duy (2001, page 18), amendments to the *Patent Act* have served to "(a) implement recommendations in a government study, (b) comply with international obligations

---

[1] A more recent history of Canadian patent law is provided by Duy (2001).

arising from trade-related agreements, and (c) improve the administration of the Act via technical and non-controversial amendments." Today, the *Patent Act* is administered by the Patent Office, which is part of the Canadian Intellectual Property Office, an agency of Industry Canada.

According to the World Intellectual Property Organization (WIPO), in 2000, there were 85,926 applications for patents in Canada, 5,518 of which were filed by residents and 80,408 of which were filed by non-residents.[2] There were only 12,125 patents granted in Canada in 2000, 1,117 of them to Canadian residents. For patents issued prior to November 19, 1987, the patent is in effect for a period of 17 years from the date of issue. For patent applications filed after November 19, 1987, the 1987 amendments to the *Patent Act* increased the term of the patent to 20 years from the date of the filing of the application in Canada.

According to Bernstein (1985), a Canadian patent document includes the following information: application number and date; issue number and date; patent classes; title of invention; name and country of residence of the inventor; name and country of residence of the patentee; priority date, country, and application number; description of the invention; and specific claims for the invention. Information on the patent, including the description of the invention, becomes available to the public when the patent is granted.[3] It is for this reason that some firms or inventors choose not to patent their inventions. They may perceive that the net benefits from maintaining the secrecy of their invention (e.g., reduced imitation of the invention) exceed the net benefits from patent protection. As a consequence, inventive output in Canada is not necessarily fully reflected by the number of patents granted in a given year.

Table 3.1 reports, for selected years, the number of Canadian and U.S. patents, and the percentage of world patents accounted for by Canadian and U.S. patents. A number of observations regarding these figures can be made: (1) the number of Canadian patents was generally increasing up to 1980, but has declined from 23,895 in 1980 to 12,125 in

---

[2] See the WIPO website at http://www.wipo.int/ipstats/en/publications/b/2000/xls/pattab1.xls.

[3] Excerpts from pages 7, 12, 29, 30, and 35 of Bernstein's article in *Technological Change in Canadian Industry* are reproduced with the permission of the Minister of Public Works and Government Services Canada, 2004, and courtesy of the Privy Council Office.

Table 3.1
Patents Granted to Canadian and U.S. Residents and Non-residents, Selected Years

| Year | Patents Granted to Canadian | | Total | Canadian Patents as |
	Residents	Non-residents	Canadian Patents	Percent of World Patents
1883	612	1,566	2,178	4.5
1900	707	3,815	4,522	5.0
1925	1,302	8,206	9,508	5.4
1950	655	7,858	8,513	5.3
1975	1,280	19,264	20,544	5.3
1980	1,503	22,392	23,895	5.7
1985	1,355	17,342	18,697	3.6
1990	1,109	13,078	14,187	2.6
1995	743	8,396	9,139	1.3
2000	1,117	11,008	12,125	1.7

| Year | Patents Granted to U.S. | | Total | U.S. Patents as |
	Residents	Non-residents	U.S. Patents	Percent of World Patents
1883			21,162	43.3
1900			24,644	27.1
1925	41,085	5,347	46,432	26.5
1950	38,721	4,408	43,129	26.7
1975	46,603	25,391	71,994	18.6
1980	37,152	24,675	61,827	14.6
1985	39,554	32,107	71,661	13.8
1990	47,393	42,973	90,366	16.4
1995	55,739	45,680	101,419	14.2
2000	85,071	72,425	157,496	22.0

Source: WIPO. 1983. *100 Years of Industrial Property Statistics*. Geneva: WIPO; WIPO website at http://www.wipo.int/ipstats/en/publications/b/2000/xls/pattabl.xls. Material provided by the World Intellectual Property Organization (WIPO), the owner of the copyright. The Secretariet of WIPO assumes no liability or responsibility with regard to the transformation of data.

2000; (2) patents granted to Canadian residents started out at 28 percent of total Canadian patents in 1883, but has declined to 9 percent of Canadian patents by 2000[4];

[4] According to Ellis and Waite (1985), in 1982 Canada granted the third highest number of patents to foreign nationals, after the United States and Britain. From this they conclude that Canada fares reasonably well in world terms as a recipient of new technology.

(3) Canadian patents as a percentage of world patents has dropped from a bit more than 5 percent through most of this century to less than 2 percent by 1995; (4) with some exceptions, the number of U.S. patents has been growing since 1883; (5) the number of patents granted to U.S. residents generally exceeds the number granted to non-residents, although the U.S. has come close to a 50-50 split since the mid-1980s; and (6) U.S. patents as a percentage of world patents has ranged from under 14 percent in 1985 to 43.3 percent in 1883, and most recently stood at around 22 percent in 2000.

It can also be observed that in 1995 and 2000, Canada granted between 0.1 and 0.2 percent of the world's total patents to its own residents, while the United States granted between 7 and 12 percent. This difference has led Ellis and Waite (1985, p. 60) to observe that "Canada is a relatively consistent but small-scale producer of new technology." Ellis and Waite also found that over the period 1972 to 1982, Canada's propensity to patent its own technology abroad remained poor compared to Germany, Britain, and the Netherlands. The ratio of the number of Canada's international patents to the number of patents granted to Canadian residents averaged around 1.50 from 1979 to 1982. This ratio is a bit lower than the corresponding ratio in France, about triple the corresponding ratio in Japan, and similar to the corresponding ratio in the U.S. for the same time period.

One expects a positive relationship between the number of patents and research and development expenditures. McFetridge (1977) found a positive relationship for the electrical, chemical and machinery industries in Canada. Other economists have found similar results for other industries. Given the relatively low level of Canada's patent activity, one might expect to observe relatively low research and development expenditures in Canada as well. This question will be examined in the next section.

III. RESEARCH AND DEVELOPMENT

Statistics Canada (2003, p. 9), in its report on business enterprise expenditures on research and development (R&D) in Canada, has obtained the following results:

Table 3.2
International Comparison of Business Enterprise R&D Expenditures, by Selected OECD Countries, 1993 to 2001

Country	Business Enterprise R&D Expenditures ÷ Gross Domestic Product (percent)		
	1993	1997	2001
Japan	1.9	2.0	2.3
Germany	1.6	1.5	1.8
United States	1.9	1.9	2.1
Sweden	2.3	2.7	3.3
France	1.5	1.4	1.4
Netherlands	1.0	1.1	1.1
Norway	0.9	0.9	1.0
Denmark	1.1	1.2	-
Canada	0.9	1.0	1.1
Italy	0.7	0.5	0.6

Source: Adapted from Table 1.1 in Statistics Canada, *Industrial Research and Development: 2003 Intentions*. Cat. No. 88-202-XIE, p. 14, December 2003. Ottawa: Minister of Industry, Science and Technology. Adapted from Table 1.1 in Statistics Canada, *Industrial Research and Development: 1997 Intentions*. Cat. No. 88-202-XPB, p. 16, 1997. Ottawa: Minister of Industry, Science and Technology.

(1) Canada's business enterprise expenditures on R&D relative to its GDP was 1.1 percent in 2001, while Japan's ratio was 2.3 percent, Germany's ratio was 1.8 percent and the United States' ratio was 2.1 percent. Table 3.2 reports the ratio of business enterprise R&D expenditure to GDP for various countries in years 1993, 1997, and 2001. Canada's ratio of R&D expenditure to GDP is similar to that of Norway and the Netherlands, and 1.8 times that of Italy.

(2) The business enterprise sector was expected to perform 54 percent of all Canadian R&D in 2002. This represents an increase from 47 percent of Canadian R&D in 1983.

(3) Between 1982 and 2001, the level of current "intramural" R&D expenditures increased at an annual rate of 8.4 percent, where intramural expenditures include "the cost of wages and salaries plus other current costs associated with workers who are usually permanent employees." However, in real terms (when the expenditures are deflated by the implicit price index of GDP), the average annual growth rate is 6.0

percent. The year 2002 represented the first year in over forty years in which intramural R&D expenditures have declined significantly.

(4) Of the 8,893 companies that reported performing R&D in 2001, 100 companies accounted for 64 percent of the R&D performed. In addition, 428 of these 8,893 companies were under foreign control, and they accounted for $4.015 billion of total R&D expenditures, representing 30 percent of total intramural R&D for 2001.

(5) R&D activities are concentrated in Ontario and Quebec. These two provinces accounted for 76 percent of R&D establishments and 85 percent of R&D expenditures for 2001.

(6) In 2001, seven industry categories accounted for 61 percent of intramural R&D expenditures, and they are as follows: communications equipment (24 percent), aerospace products and parts (7 percent), scientific research and development services (4 percent), information and cultural industries (5 percent), semiconductor and other electronic equipment (7 percent), pharmaceutical and medicine (7 percent), and computer system design and related services (7 percent).

The recent figures on Canada's R&D expenditures seem to continue earlier trends reported by Bernstein (1985). He found that over the period 1971 to 1981, R&D expenditures in current dollars increased by 223 percent, and R&D expenditures in 1971 dollars increased by more than 31 percent. The ratio of R&D expenditure to GDP fell from a high in 1971 of 1.36 percent to a low in 1976 of 1.06 percent, and climbed back up to 1.28 percent in 1981. The business enterprise sector comprised 51 percent of R&D expenditures in the non-government sector in 1971 and 63 percent in 1981. The non-government sector accounted for 75 percent of all R&D in 1981. With respect to the regional distribution of R&D expenditures, Ontario and Quebec accounted for 71 percent of Canadian R&D expenditures in 1981.

Given Canada's relatively low level of R&D expenditures compared to other OECD countries and its major trading partners, economists have been concerned with the determinants of R&D. Cumming and MacIntosh (2000) studied the determinants of R&D for 56 firms in the Canadian biotechnology industry using survey data. The authors found that firms that ranked patent protection as important in determining R&D spending had higher R&D expenditures (as a ratio of total expenditures) than other firms. Firms that pursue platform technologies allocate a smaller proportion of total expenditures to R&D, as do firms with greater debt-equity ratios. Finally, and unexpectedly, R&D spending as a ratio of total expenditures was higher for firms engaged in areas of research that are considered controversial. The authors provided several possible interpretations for this result.

Tang and Rao (2003) used a data set on Canadian-controlled firms and foreign-controlled firms over the 1985 to 1994 period to study the effects of nationality of ownership, firm size, industry composition, and export orientation on R&D intensity. The authors found that once other factors are controlled for, foreign-controlled firms were less R&D intensive than Canadian-controlled firms, despite being significantly more productive. The authors interpreted this finding as suggesting that foreign-controlled firms received important R&D transfers from their parent companies.

In another study, Betts et al. (2001) examined the role of unions in determining R&D expenditure. Data on a number of variables, including R&D expenditures as a ratio of GDP, for 13 industries over the 1968 to 1986 time period were used. The authors found that, controlling for other factors, an increase in the rate of unionization in an industry was negatively related to R&D intensity. The authors concluded that this finding supports the hypothesis that union rent seeking reduces R&D investment.

Another focus of research has been the effect of government grant and tax policies on R&D expenditure. Howe and McFetridge (1976) studied the R&D expenditures of 81 firms in the Canadian electrical, chemical, and machinery industries over the period 1967 to 1971 and concluded that the principal determinants of R&D expenditures were sales, cash flow, and government grants. More specifically, they found that R&D incentive grants had a statistically significant effect on R&D expenditure only in the electrical industry, and that Canadian-owned firms increased their R&D expenditures by more than the amount of the grant, while foreign-owned firms increased their R&D expenditures by less than the amount of the grant. The condition of the domestic financial environment was found to be less relevant in explaining the variation in R&D expenditures among foreign-owned firms than it is in explaining the variation in R&D expenditures among Canadian-owned firms. Howe and McFetridge suggested that this result implied that the R&D decision of foreign-owned firms might not be made in a strictly Canadian context.

Bernstein (1985) has noted that the federal government has used various types of grants to encourage R&D investment. For example, the Industrial Research Assistance Program was established in 1968 and was available to companies incorporated in Canada that undertook R&D investment and product development innovation in Canada. The Defence Industry Productivity Program was established in 1968 and was designed to encourage R&D investment into product and process development in the defence industries. Other federal programs have also been created to promote R&D in Canada. Bernstein (1985, p. 30) has been somewhat critical of the available empirical work relating to R&D expenditure and government grants.[5] From his review of the literature, he concluded that there was evidence that grants led firms to increase their R&D expenditure.

With respect to tax incentives and R&D, Bernstein (1985, p. 35) concluded that there was evidence that tax incentives had positive effects on R&D expenditure. On balance, tax incentives appeared to generate one dollar of additional R&D expenditure for every dollar decrease in tax revenue.[6] Different results have been obtained by Mansfield and Switzer (1985). They conducted a survey of 55 firms and obtained estimates of the effects of two direct R&D tax incentives (the investment tax credit and the special research allowance) on each firm's R&D expenditure in 1980, 1981, 1982, and 1983. They found that the special research allowance increased R&D expenditure by about one percent, the investment tax credit increased R&D expenditure by about two percent, and that these increases amounted to about 30 or 40 percent of the revenue losses to the government. Bernstein (1986) suggested that one reason that their results differ from his results might be that with the survey one has to depend upon persons to reveal what their companies would have done if circumstances had been different.

---

[5] Bernstein (1985, p. 30) noted that (1) the different types of grants have not been differentiated in the empirical results, (2) grants have been related to R&D expenditure rather than to the stock of knowledge, so that intertemporal influences of grants on R&D capital have been ignored, and (3) the empirical models have assumed that the determinants of the demand for R&D capital are independent of the determinants of the demand for physical capital and labour.

[6] Bernstein (1986, p. 445), in his study of the effect of direct and indirect tax incentives on Canadian industrial R&D expenditures, has concluded that "The results show that both the R&D tax credit and allowance generate approximately $.80 of additional R&D expenditures per dollar cost to the government, when output production in the economy is constant. Once the effects of output expansion are included, R&D expenditures generally increase by more than the foregone tax revenues due to the direct incentives." With respect to an indirect tax incentive, like the business investment tax credit, "even in terms of a dollar of foregone tax revenues, the indirect tax incentive causes R&D expenditures to increase by about 10 percent of the increase arising from the direct tax incentives on R&D investment."

Economists have addressed two other Canadian R&D issues, and these are R&D spillovers and technology diffusion. With respect to the former, Bernstein (1988) used data from seven industries for the years 1978 to 1981 to estimate the effects of R&D spillovers on the costs and structure of production of the receiving firms. The social rates of return to R&D investment and the deviations from the private rate of return were also estimated. He found that both intraindustry and interindustry spillovers reduced the average costs of production, but unit costs declined more due to interindustry spillovers than to intraindustry spillovers. R&D spillovers caused the social and private rates of return to R&D investment to differ. He found that the social rate of return exceeded the private rate of return by 70 (115) percent in industries with relatively small (large) R&D spending propensities. These results would tend to support government tax and grant policies that are designed to encourage more R&D expenditure by firms.

Finally, McFetridge and Corvari (1985) have surveyed the literature on technology diffusion, particularly as it relates to Canada. They cited the work of Globerman who found that the adoption of new technologies in Canada proceeded more slowly than in the U.S. McFetridge and Corvari also stated that the evidence (largely obtained by Globerman) tends to show that early adoption of new technologies is facilitated by larger firm size, R&D expenditures, foreign ownership, and various measures of organizational receptivity to change. They also found that the transfer lag of new technology to Canada does not differ, on average, from the transfer lag to other industrial countries. McFetridge and Corvari concluded their analysis by noting that while there have been government programs devoted to promoting diffusion of technology, a better understanding of the diffusion process would enable government to design more appropriate programs.

IV. PATENT POLICY AND THE PHARMACEUTICAL INDUSTRY IN CANADA

One of the most controversial aspects of Canadian patent policy relates to compulsory licensing for pharmaceuticals. Compulsory licensing for pharmaceuticals was in effect in Canada between 1923 and 1993. However, until 1969, licenses could only be issued for the manufacture, use and sale of patented processes in connection with pharmaceuticals. In 1969, the Canadian *Patent Act* was amended to allow for compulsory licensing to import patented pharmaceutical products. The Commissioner of Patents set the royalty rate at four percent of the licensee's selling price. That is, once a four percent royalty was paid, a license could be obtained to manufacture and/or sell a patented drug. As noted by

Gorecki and Henderson (1981), the licensee would sell in competition with the patentee exactly the same drug, but under a different name. The licensee's drugs are sometimes referred to as generic drugs. Gorecki and Henderson also pointed out that the objective of the amendment to the *Patent Act* was to reduce drug prices in Canada by weakening patent protection for drugs and stimulating competition from the licensees. Fowler (1984) has further noted that the rationale behind the amendment appears to be that the pharmaceutical industry in Canada was perceived to be dominated by non-Canadian firms. Canadian consumers were paying higher prices than consumers in other countries, so that Canadians were in effect paying excessive monopoly rents on non-Canadian inventions. "Foreign, rather than indigenous innovators and entrepreneurs were being rewarded by the Canadian patent system" (Fowler, 1984, p. 64).

In April 1984, Harry C. Eastman was appointed Commissioner under Part I of the *Inquiries Act* "to inquire into and report upon the current situation in the pharmaceutical industry in Canada, the prospects for a significant expansion of this industry in Canada and the policy framework for the development of the pharmaceutical industry and, within that framework, to identify proposals that might form the basis for reaching a consensus on licensing policy."[7] As part of that inquiry, the Commission found that sales of 70 compulsorily licensed drugs in Canada amounted to $328 million out of a total of $1.6 billion for all ethical drugs in 1983. Generic firms sold and paid royalties on 32 of the 70 compulsorily licensed drugs, and their sales of these drugs amounted to $46 million or 21 percent of the $217 million in total sales for these drugs. The generic firms also accounted for 34 percent of the volume of compulsorily licensed drugs. The discrepancy between the generic firms' sales value and sales volume shares was due to the fact that generic firms charge prices that are approximately half those of patentees. The sales of compulsorily licensed drugs by generic firms amounted to three percent of total sales of pharmaceuticals in Canada in 1983.

Gorecki (1986) reported that between 1969 (the year in which the *Patent Act* was amended) and 1983, 181 compulsory patent licenses had been taken out against 58 drugs by approximately 30 firms or licensees. Of these 181 licenses, only 66 were being worked in 1983. Of the top 50 selling drugs in Canada in January 1983, 21 faced competition from at least one licensee.

---

[7] See Commission of Inquiry on the Pharmaceutical Industry (1985, p. 1).

Two of the issues that the Commission of Inquiry on the Pharmaceutical Industry had to address were the effects of compulsory licensing of pharmaceuticals on the prices of licensed pharmaceuticals and on Canadian pharmaceutical R&D expenditures. Earlier, between 1976 and 1979, the Pharmaceutical Manufacturers Association of Canada (PMAC) had released a number of documents presenting their views on these matters. Gorecki and Henderson (1981) summarized PMAC's view as being that compulsory licensing has not led to price reductions at the manufacturing or retail level and compulsory licensing has adversely affected R&D in the drug industry.[8] Gorecki and Henderson disagreed with PMAC's views, and argued that (1) "prices have declined at the manufacturing level and in differing degrees at the level of the consumer," and (2) "given the multinational nature of most of the major drug patentees, the international nature of the industry, the overall trends in R&D for Canadian industry, then the relationship between compulsory licensing in Canada and the levelling off and slight decline of R&D on drugs is at best unproved and hence of relatively minor adverse consequence compared to the other factors mentioned."

Fowler (1984) has calculated the average Canadian price paid by pharmacists for a sample of drugs for which compulsory licenses were issued for three selected years: 1968 (before the *Patent Act* was amended), 1976 (chosen because it allowed sufficient time to elapse since the *Patent Act* was amended), and 1980 (the most recent year for which he had price data). He then compared these prices with the corresponding prices paid by U.S. pharmacists. He concluded that compulsory licensing combined with provincial product selection legislation (which requires pharmacists to substitute cheaper for more expensive drugs that are deemed to be equivalent) has had the effect of reducing the manufacturers' average price of compulsorily licensed drugs sold to the pharmacist in Canada from about 86 percent of the U.S. price in 1968 to 45 percent of the U.S. price in 1980.

Hartle (1984) was skeptical that any of the policy changes with respect to compulsory licensing being considered by Consumer and Corporate Affairs Canada in 1983 would result in an increase in R&D in the pharmaceutical industry in Canada. The alternatives to price competition through compulsory licensing of inputs being considered were price monitoring with sanctions if prices exceed stated guidelines, variable royalty rates, a

---

[8] According to Hartle (1984, p. 81), PMAC was willing to admit in a brief dated February 1983 that "compulsory licensing had reduced some drug prices (slightly, in their view)."

fixed period of patent exclusivity on an industry basis, and company-specific exemptions from compulsory licenses. In Hartle's view, the multinational drug companies operating in Canada found that it was more efficient to carry out their R&D at their parents' facilities outside Canada. While the alternatives to compulsory licensing might lead to more Canadian R&D by a multinational's Canadian subsidiary (in order to qualify for greater patent protection and higher prices for longer periods), and possibly the discovery of a new drug, there is no assurance that the benefits would accrue to Canada rather than to the parent company and/or the home country of the parent. Hartle concluded his discussion by stating that there is little reason to believe that the price, R&D, value added in manufacturing, and employment performance of the multinationals would be better after the repeal of compulsory licensing of pharmaceuticals than it was before the *Patent Act* was amended to allow it in 1969.

Apparently, the Commission of Inquiry on the Pharmaceutical Industry (1985) was also of the opinion that compulsory licensing of pharmaceuticals and the subsequent competition from generic drug producers have resulted in lower pharmaceutical prices in Canada. Furthermore, the Commission was of the opinion that "Compulsory licensing has not had a discernible negative impact on the profitability and rate of growth of the pharmaceutical industry in Canada as a whole."[9] The Commission recommended that compulsory licensing be retained, but that new drugs should receive a period of exclusivity from generic competition of four years after receiving their Notice of Compliance authorizing marketing. The period of exclusivity was intended to allow the innovating firm to develop its sales and cover its costs, including the promotion costs of a new drug. The Commission also recommended that the royalty arrangements be modified to increase payments of generic firms to the patent-holding firms so as to further compensate the patent-holding firms for their research and development expenditures.

---

[9] Commission of Inquiry on the Pharmaceutical Industry (1985, p. 7).

In November 1987, section 41(4) of the *Patent Act* was amended by Bill C-22 but not quite in the way envisaged by the Commission of Inquiry on the Pharmaceutical Industry. Instead of four years, Bill C-22 allowed a period of exclusivity of seven to ten years to patent-holding firms before a compulsory license could be issued for their products.[10] According to the Patented Medicine Prices Review Board (2002, p. 29), with the adoption of Bill C-22, Canada's research based pharmaceutical companies made a commitment that the brand name pharmaceutical industry would increase its annual R&D expenditures as a percentage of sales to 10 percent by 1996.

More recently, the *Patent Act* was amended on February 15, 1993, by Bill C-91. This bill implemented the federal government's new policy of having pharmaceutical patents accorded the same treatment as all other patents. According to Blakney (1993) compulsory pharmaceutical patent licenses issued before December 20, 1991, will continue in effect (subject to the conditions established in the 1987 revision to the *Patent Act*). Any compulsory license that was granted on or after December 20, 1991 was deemed to have no effect.

Bill C-91 also retained the Patented Medicine Prices Review Board (PMPRB) that had been established by the 1987 amendment to the *Patent Act* to prevent excessive patented pharmaceutical prices and to report to the government on price and R&D trends, but its powers were changed.[11] Since compulsory licensing was eliminated, the Board can no longer use the removal of patent exclusivity and the requirement of a compulsory license as a remedy against excessive pharmaceutical prices. The Board retains its ability to make prospective price orders (i.e., to order that the price of a patented pharmaceutical not exceed a level considered by the Board to be excessive). Blakney (1993) also reported that the Board has been given the power to order a patentee to give up the

---

[10] This was noted by Anis (1992, p. 421). Anis studied the effect of formularies on the pricing of generic pharmaceuticals. A formulary is a catalogue of pharmaceutical products and their prices and indicates which pharmaceuticals are interchangeable.

[11] The Board consists of five members, appointed by the Governor in Council, having a maximum of two five-year terms. The Board has all of the powers of a superior court.

revenues generated from the excessive portion of the price of the medicine in the past.[12]

The government has thus moved from compulsory licensing as a means of keeping pharmaceutical prices in check to a system of price monitoring and (if necessary) price regulation. Several studies have examined the effects that the 1987 and 1993 amendments to the *Patent Act* have had on pharmaceutical prices and R&D in Canada. With respect to R&D, Pazderka (1999) has examined the impact of the 1987 amendments on pharmaceutical industry R&D spending in Canada. He found that R&D spending by PMAC members accelerated after 1988, but that a slowdown in the rate of growth occurred in the 1994 to 1997 period. The commitment to raise the R&D to sales ratio to 10 percent by 1996 was met in 1993. Pazderka concluded (on p. 43) that the preponderance of data analysis and statistical tests presented in his paper support the conclusion that the tightening of patent protection in Bill C-22 led to a change in trend in pharmaceutical R&D spending in Canada, but that the increase should not be attributed exclusively to the economics of patent protection. Part of the increase can likely be attributed to the commitment made by PMAC members to increase R&D spending.

In its 2002 Annual Report (p. 27), the PMPRB summarised the results of its study comparing R&D spending by the brand name pharmaceutical industry in Canada and other major industrialized countries (i.e., France, Germany, Italy, Sweden, Switzerland, the United Kingdom, and the United States). The analysis covered the period 1995 to 2000. The PMPRB found that while R&D spending in Canada increased 51 percent from $626 million in 1995 to $945 million in 2000, Canada still ranked behind other industrialized countries by several measures. In particular, the R&D to sales ratio in

---

[12] According to section 85 of the amended *Patent Act*, in determining whether a medicine is being or has been sold at an excessive price in Canada, the Board shall take into consideration the following factors to the extent information on the factors is available to the Board: (i) the prices at which the medicine has been sold in the relevant market, (ii) the prices at which other medicines in the same therapeutic class have been sold in the relevant market, (iii) the prices at which the medicine and other medicines in the same therapeutic class have been sold in countries other than Canada, (iv) changes in the Consumer Price Index, and (v) such other factors as may be specified in any regulation made for the purposes of this subsection. If the Board finds that a patentee's prices were excessive, the Board may (under section 83 of the amended *Patent Act*) direct the patentee to (i) reduce the price at which the patentee sells the medicine in any market in Canada, to such extent and for such period as specified in the order, (ii) reduce the price at which the patentee sells one other medicine to which a patented invention of the patentee pertains in any market in Canada, to such extent and for such period as is specified in the order, or (iii) pay to Her Majesty in right of Canada an amount specified in the order.

Canada was 10.1 percent in 2000, while the aggregate ratio for the seven industrialized countries was 19.0 percent. The PMPRB also looked at R&D spending relative to population and GDP and it found low levels of pharmaceutical R&D spending in Canada compared to the other countries examined. In terms of composition, 55.6 percent of pharmaceutical R&D spending in Canada in 2002 was on applied research (e.g., pre-clinical and clinical trials and addressing problems in the manufacturing process).

With respect to pharmaceutical pricing, Jones et al. (2001) examined the impact of the 1987 changes in the *Patent Act* on the pricing of prescription drugs. Jones et al. expected the increased patent protection provided by the 1987 amendments to reduce competition that the branded pharmaceutical firms faced from generic competitors, thus allowing prices to increase. Using price data on a sample of 82 drugs from the British Columbia Pharmacare Programme for the period 1981 to1994, they found that generics succeeded in reducing market prices (both brand and generic) prior to 1987. They concluded that after 1987, the effectiveness of generic competition was reduced, and notwithstanding the activities of the PMPRB, both branded and market prices of pharmaceuticals increased. Jones et al. suggested that the government should consider amending the patent laws once again to reduce restrictions on generic entry.

To monitor the trends in manufacturers' prices of patented drugs, the PMPRB calculates a Patented Medicine Price Index (PMPI). According to the PMPRB (2002, p. 21), "This index measures average year-over-year changes in the transaction prices of patented drug products sold in Canada based on the price and sales information reported by patentees." The PMPRB found that this index fell by 1.2 percent in 2002, and that this continues the "pattern of declines and near negligible increases in the PMPI that began in 1993." However, consistent with the findings of Jones et al. (2001), the PMPRB reported that the PMPI did register increases from 1988 to 1993.

Finally, on a related pharmaceutical patent policy topic, Hollis (2003) has examined the implications of allowing brand-name pharmaceutical firms in Canada to license a "pseudo-generic" company to compete directly against other generic firms. The pseudo-generic firm is owned by the brand-name firm, and produces a product that is identical to the one supplied by the brand-name firm. Hollis argued that the use of pseudo-generics has the potential to eliminate competition in medium-sized markets where the potential profits are not large enough to support multiple generics, and it likely delays entry in other markets. Hollis suggested several possible remedies for this situation, including one that would prohibit brand name pharmaceutical companies from licensing pseudo-generics unless they stopped producing the brand-name version of the drug.

V. SUMMARY

In this chapter, some data on Canada's patent performance and research and development expenditures have been presented. It was found that the number of patents granted to Canadian residents is small relative to the number of Canadian patents granted in a given year (i.e., 9 percent of total Canadian patents in 2000), and that Canadian patents as a percentage of world patents has dropped in recent years. Canada's propensity to patent its own technology abroad is regarded as weak and the overall level of Canada's patent activity is regarded as low.

Consistent with Canada's level of patent activity is its R&D effort. Canada's R&D expenditure relative to its GDP was approximately half the ratio of Japan, Germany, and the U.S. Government grants and tax incentives have been found to have positive effects on research and development expenditure in Canada, and these can be partly justified by the R&D spillovers that have been found to exist in Canada.

One of the most controversial aspects of Canadian patent policy relates to compulsory licensing to import patented pharmaceutical products. The purpose of such licensing was to reduce drug prices in Canada by weakening patent protection for drugs (largely discovered outside of Canada), and stimulating competition from the licensees. There is evidence that compulsory licensing lowered drug prices in Canada, and there is little evidence that it adversely affected R&D in the Canadian pharmaceutical industry. Nonetheless, the Government of Canada has eliminated compulsory licensing for pharmaceuticals. There is some evidence that Canada's changes in patent policy for pharmaceuticals have led to increases in Canadian pharmaceutical R&D and higher pharmaceutical prices as well.

REFERENCES

Anis, Aslam. 1992. "Pharmaceutical Prices with Insurance Coverage and Formularies," *Canadian Journal of Economics* 25: 420–437.

Bernstein, Jeffrey I. 1985. "Research and Development, Patents, and Grant and Tax Policies in Canada," in Donald G. McFetridge, ed., *Technological Change in Canadian Industry*. Toronto: University of Toronto Press.

Bernstein, Jeffrey I. 1986. "The Effect of Direct and Indirect Tax Incentives on Canadian Industrial R&D Expenditures," *Canadian Public Policy* 12: 438–448.

Bernstein, Jeffrey I. 1988. "Costs of Production, Intra– and Interindustry R&D Spillovers: Canadian Evidence," *Canadian Journal of Economics* 21: 324–340.

Betts, Julian, Cameron Odgers, and Michael Wilson. 2001. "The Effects of Unions on Research and Development: An Empirical Analysis using Multi–year Data," *Canadian Journal of Economics* 34: 785–806.

Blakney, John F. 1993. "Pharmaceutical Patent Right Revisions Take Effect," *Canadian Competition Record* 14: 43–47.

Commission of Inquiry on the Pharmaceutical Industry. 1985. *Summary of the Report of the Commission of Inquiry on the Pharmaceutical Industry*. Ottawa: Minister of Supply and Services Canada.

Cumming, Douglas and Jeffrey MacIntosh. 2000. "The Determinants of R&D Expenditures: A Study of the Canadian Biotechnology Industry," *Review of Industrial Organization* 17: 357–370.

Duy, Vic. 2001. "A Brief History of the Canadian Patent System." Canadian Biotechnology Advisory Committee research paper.

Economic Council of Canada. 1971. *Report on Intellectual and Industrial Property*. Ottawa: Government of Canada.

Ellis, Ned and David Waite. 1985. "Canadian Technological Output in a World Context," in Donald G. McFetridge, ed., *Technological Change in Canadian Industry*. Toronto: University of Toronto Press.

Fowler, David J. 1984. "The Effect of Public Policy Initiatives on Drug Prices in Canada," *Canadian Public Policy* 10: 64–73.

Gorecki, Paul K. 1986. "The Importance of Being First: The Case of Prescription Drugs in Canada," *International Journal of Industrial Organization* 4: 371–395.

Gorecki, Paul K. and Ida Henderson. 1981. "Compulsory Patent Licensing of Drugs in Canada: A Comment on the Debate," *Canadian Public Policy* 7: 559–568.

Hartle, Douglas G. 1984. "Federal Proposals to Restrict Competition in the Canadian Pharmaceutical Industry," *Canadian Public Policy* 10: 81–87.

Hollis, Aidan. 2003. "The Anti–Competitive Effects of Brand–Controlled "Pseudo–Generics" in the Canadian Pharmaceutical Market," *Canadian Public Policy* 29: 21–32.

Howe, J.D. and McFetridge, D.G. 1976. "The Determinants of R&D Expenditures," *Canadian Journal of Economics* 9: 57–71.

Jones, J.C.H., Tanya Potashnik, and Anming Zhang. 2001. "Patents, Brand-Generic Competition and the Pricing of Ethical Drugs in Canada: Some Empirical Evidence from British Columbia, 1981–1994," *Applied Economics* 33: 947–956.

Mansfield, Edwin and Lorne Switzer. 1985. "How Effective Are Canada's Direct Tax Incentives for R&D?," *Canadian Public Policy* 11: 241–246.

McFetridge, Donald G. 1977. *Government Support of Scientific Research and Development: An Economic Analysis*. Toronto: Ontario Economic Council.

McFetridge, D.G. and R.J. Corvari. 1985. "Technology Diffusion: A Survey of Canadian Evidence and Public Policy Issues," in D.G. McFetridge, ed., *Technological Change in Canadian Industry*. Toronto: University of Toronto Press.

Patented Medicine Prices Review Board. 2002. *PMPRB 2002 Annual Report.* Ottawa: PMPRB. Patented Medicine Prices Review Board—Annual Report 2002 (www.pmprb-cepmb.gc.ca) © Her Majesty the Queen in Right of Canada. Reproduced and adapted with the permission of the Minister of Public Works and Government Services Canada, 2004, on behalf of the Patented Medicine Prices Review Board.

Pazderka, Bohumir. 1999. "Patent Protection and Pharmaceutical R&D Spending in Canada," *Canadian Public Policy* 25: 29–46.

Statistics Canada. 1997. *Industrial Research and Development: 1997 Intentions*. Cat. No. 88–202–XPB.

Statistics Canada. 2003. *Industrial Research and Development: 2003 Intentions*. Cat. No. 88–202–XIE. Ottawa: Minister of Industry.

Tang, Jianmin and Someshwar Rao. 2003. "Are Foreign–Controlled Manufacturing Firms Less R&D–Intensive than Canadian–Controlled Firms?" *Canadian Public Policy* 29: 111–117.

CHAPTER 4

COMPETITION POLICY IN CANADA

I. HISTORY OF COMPETITION POLICY IN CANADA[1]

In 1889, one year before the passage of the U.S. Sherman Act, Canada's Parliament passed *An Act for the Prevention and Suppression of Combinations Found in Restraint of Trade*. Section 1 of this Act made it a criminal offence to conspire, combine, agree, or arrange to limit unduly facilities for transporting, producing, manufacturing, supplying, storing, or selling any article, or to restrain commerce in it, or to unreasonably enhance its price, or to prevent or lessen competition in the production, manufacture, purchase, barter, sale, transportation or supply of any such article or commodity. This section of the Act was moved to the Criminal Code in 1892, and it remained there until the *Combines Investigation Act* was consolidated in 1960.[2]

One major weakness recognized in the original Act was that it did not create any investigative machinery for violations of the Act. This was remedied to some extent by the passage of the *Combines Investigation Act* of 1910. This Act allowed the Minister of Labour to appoint ad hoc boards that could compel attendance of witnesses and production of documents. The Act also contained a provision that allowed six citizens to apply to a superior court judge for an order directing an investigation into an alleged combine. A combine under the Act included a merger, a trust, and a monopoly. To be unlawful, the combination, merger, trust or monopoly must have operated or be likely to operate to the detriment or against the interest of the public, whether consumers, producers or others.

In 1919, Parliament passed the *Board of Commerce Act*, which set up a Board of Commerce consisting of three commissioners to administer another new act, *The Combines and Fair Prices Act*. (These acts replaced the *Combines Investigation Act* of 1910.) This legislation ran into constitutional problems and was replaced by a new *Combines Investigation Act* in 1923. The Act provided for the appointment of a Registrar who would administer the Act. The Registrar could hold a preliminary

---

[1] This review of the history of competition policy in Canada is based on material in Dunlop, McQueen, and Trebilcock (1987, Ch. 3) and Economic Council of Canada (1969, Ch. 4).

[2] See Economic Council of Canada (1969, pp. 51–52).

inquiry on her own initiative, on formal application of six persons, or on ministerial direction.

In 1935, the Criminal Code was amended with the inclusion of a section dealing with price discrimination and predatory pricing. This action was taken in response to the *Report of the Royal Commission on Price Spreads* (1935), and to the concern that large firms were able to obtain discounts on the purchase of supplies that smaller competitors were unable to obtain. The price discrimination section was transferred to the *Combines Investigation Act* in 1960.

Parliament, in 1937, chose to place investigations under the *Combines Investigation Act* in the hands of a commissioner. The commissioner, according to the Economic Council of Canada (1969, p. 55), "was empowered to compel the attendance of witnesses, secure testimony under oath and require the production of documents." However, a concern raised by the MacQuarrie Committee (set up in 1950 to study the purposes and methods of the *Combines Investigation Act*) that the commissioner was placed in the position of both prosecutor and judge led Parliament to amend the *Combines Investigation Act*. The commissioner's powers were placed in the hands of a Director of Investigation and Research, who could initiate inquiries and conduct investigations, and a Restrictive Trade Practices Commission (consisting of not more than three members appointed by the Governor in Council) that could authorize seizure of documents, the oral examination of witnesses, and orders for written returns. The Commission was also to hear and appraise evidence presented to it by the Director as well as any other evidence it deemed necessary to ensure that persons under investigation were heard, and was to report to the Minister of Justice.

The MacQuarrie Committee, in its Interim Report dated October 1951, had also recommended that resale price maintenance be made an offence under the Act. Parliament agreed and passed an amendment making it an offence to fix minimum resale prices (although suggested retail prices were still allowed).

In 1960, the *Combines Investigation Act* was once again amended. The Criminal Code provisions dealing with conspiracies, mergers and monopolies were brought into the Act. In doing so, the word "trust" was eliminated and separate provisions were created "defining mergers and monopolies and making them offences only where they were likely to be, or to operate, to the detriment or against the interest of the public."[3]

The Economic Council of Canada issued its *Interim Report on Competition Policy* in July 1969. While it recommended that a number of practices be more strictly prohibited by the criminal law (i.e., collusive arrangements, resale price maintenance, and misleading advertising), it also recommended that mergers and monopolies, along with refusing to deal, exclusive dealing, tied selling, price discrimination, and predatory practices, be made matters reviewable by a civil tribunal. The first bill, Bill C-256, introduced by the government in 1971 to revise competition policy in response to the Economic Council's report did not pass. In 1975, the so-called Stage I amendments did pass. One amendment extended the *Combines Investigation Act*, which had previously applied only to goods, to all services. Bid rigging was made a separate per se offence. The Restrictive Trade Practices Commission was given the power to review and prohibit refusals to deal, consignment selling, exclusive dealing, market restriction, and tied selling. The Act was also amended to allow an individual to sue for damages where the person has suffered loss or damage as a result of conduct that is contrary to the Act or the failure of any person to comply with an order of the Commission or a court under the Act. Finally, the Director was given the authority, at the request of any federal board, commission, or other tribunal or on his own initiative, to make representations to and call evidence before the board, commission, or tribunal in respect of competition.[4]

Stage II amendments to the *Combines Investigation Act* were introduced as Bill C-13 in March 1977. The bill proposed treating mergers as a matter of civil law, and allowing the Competition Policy Advocate (who would replace the Director) to challenge before the Competition Board (that would replace the Restrictive Trade Practices Commission) those mergers that entail a substantial lessening of competition.[5] Bill C-13 did not pass.

Another attempt to reform competition policy was made in 1984 with the introduction of Bill C-29, but it did not pass before the change from a Liberal to a Conservative government in 1984. It was a Conservative bill, Bill C-91, introduced in 1985, that

---

[3] See Economic Council of Canada (1969, p. 61).

[4] See Dunlop, McQueen, and Trebilcock (1987, pp. 52–54); reproduced with the permission of Canada Law Book Inc. (1-800-263-3269, www.canadalawbook.ca).

[5] For a review and analysis of the Stage II amendments, see Rowley and Stanbury (1978).

eventually passed in 1986. The name of the *Combines Investigation Act* was changed to the *Competition Act*, and the *Competition Tribunal Act* set up a Competition Tribunal to replace the Restrictive Trade Practices Commission.

The purpose of the *Competition Act*, as stated in section 1.1, is "to maintain and encourage competition in Canada in order to promote the efficiency and adaptability of the Canadian economy, in order to expand opportunities for Canadian participation in world markets while at the same time recognizing the role of foreign competition in Canada, in order to ensure that small and medium-sized enterprises have an equitable opportunity to participate in the Canadian economy and in order to provide consumers with competitive prices and product choices."

The *Competition Act* incorporated the following important changes to the *Combines Investigation Act*:[6] (a) a strengthening of the cartel (conspiracy) provisions, (b) the addition of state-owned corporations and banks to the set of firms covered by the Act, (c) the addition of provisions empowering the Competition Tribunal to approve specialization agreements that provide for the rationalization of product lines among competitors, (d) a number of practices, including refusal to deal, consignment selling, exclusive dealing, tied selling, market restriction, abuse of dominant position, delivered pricing, and merger, are made civilly reviewable by the Competition Tribunal, and (e) mergers above a certain size threshold must be reported in advance to the Director.

With respect to the Competition Tribunal, it shall consist of not more than four members to be appointed from among the judges of the Federal Court-Trial Division by the Governor in Council on the recommendation of the Minister of Justice, and not more than eight other members to be appointed by the Governor in Council on the recommendation of the Minister. The Governor in Council shall designate one of the judicial members to be Chairman of the Tribunal, and each judicial member shall be appointed for a term not exceeding seven years and holds office so long as he/she remains a judge of the Federal Court. Each lay member of the Tribunal shall also be appointed for a term not exceeding seven years.

The Tribunal has jurisdiction to hear and determine all applications under Part VIII of the *Competition Act*. The Tribunal is a court of record, and has certain judicial powers

---

[6] See Trebilcock (1990, pp. 56) for a more detailed discussion of these changes.

with respect to the attendance, swearing, and examination of witnesses, the production and inspection of documents, and the enforcement of its orders. No fewer than three and no more than five members shall hear each application to the Tribunal, at least one of whom is a judicial member and one of whom is a lay member. In proceedings before the Tribunal, only the judicial members sitting in those proceedings shall determine questions of law; all members sitting in those proceedings shall determine questions of fact or mixed law and fact. Decisions or orders of the Tribunal may be appealed to the Federal Court of Appeal.

One might expect that with the creation of the reviewable practices section of the *Competition Act*, enforcement of competition law would be improved and more competition cases would be observed. The enforcement of competition law in Canada will be reviewed in the next section.

II. ENFORCEMENT OF COMPETITION LAW IN CANADA

Gorecki and Stanbury (1979) have undertaken an exhaustive analysis of every complaint, discontinued inquiry, Restrictive Trade Practices Commission report, case referred directly to the Department of Justice but not prosecuted and every prosecution which began in the period 1960-1975. They also examined the record of enforcement for the period 1889-1959. The results of their investigation, updated to 1991 by material found in Stanbury (1991) and the Annual Reports of the Director of Investigation and Research, appear in Table 4.1.[7] Recent years are not included be-

---

[7] Misleading advertising and deceptive marketing practice cases are excluded from Table 4.1. Practices prohibited by the *Competition Act* include (a) representations which are false or misleading in a material respect, (b) performance claims not based on adequate and proper tests, (c) misleading representations as to the price at which a product is ordinarily sold, (d) advertising a product at a bargain price, where the advertiser does not have the product available in reasonable quantities, (e) supplying a product at a price higher than the price which is currently being advertised by the vendor, (f) and conducting a promotional contest, unless there is adequate and fair disclosure of the number and approximate value of prizes, and of material information relating to the chances of winning. Other provisions of the Act deal with warranties, tests and testimonials, double ticketing and pyramid and referral selling.

The Bureau maintains a high level of activity under the misleading advertising and deceptive marketing practices provisions of the Act. In the fiscal year ended March 31, 2003, the Bureau received 18,411 complaints regarding fair business practices under the *Competition Act*, and commenced inquiries in 26 new cases under the Act. Criminal charges were laid in 10 cases. Total fines and administrative monetary penalties under the *Competition Act* were $860,850.

Table 4.1
Competition Cases and Activities, 1888–1991

| Period, Fiscal Year Ending March 31 | Total | Combines Prosecutions[1] | | | | Reports or Cases Sent to Attorney General but not Prosecuted | Discon- tinued Inquiries | Files Opened in Response to Complaints |
		Con- spiracy[2]	Merger and/or Monopoly	RPM and Re- fusal to Sell	Other			
1889–1910	10	10	0	na	0	na	na	na
1911–1923	1	1	0	na	0	na	na	na
1924–1940	13	10	1	na	2	17	na	538
1941–1946	3	3	0	na	0	0	na	66
1947–1955	9	6	1	2	0	9	25[5]	794[6]
1956–1960	18	13	2	1	2	6	30	456
1961–1965	19	8	0	10	1	10	77	816
1966–1970	25	16	1	7	1	5	82	579
1971–1975	45	18	4	15	8	19	95	963
1976–1980	72	19	2	47	4	19	74	941[7]
1981–1985	82	18	0	58	6	26	96	1147
1986–1989	63[3]	21	2[4]	38	3	19	71	1152[8]
1990–1991	16	8	0[4]	6	2	2	15	748

na = data not available. [1]Excludes all misleading advertising and deceptive marketing practices cases and 3 patent cases started in 1945/46, 1967/68 and 1969/70. [2]Dated by month in which the case was completed. [3]Excludes merger cases. [4]This excludes civil law merger and abuse of dominant position cases brought under the *Competition Act* of 1986. [5]1951–1955 only. [6]1950/51– 1954/55 only (542). [7]1957–1982 figures cover "substantive complaints only, due to change in procedure in Records Office." This changes to "files which required two or more days of review" beginning in 1982–83. [8]Includes merger cases.

Source: Stanbury (1991) for years 1889–1989 and the *Annual Reports of the Director of Investigation and Research* for 1990–1991.

cause of the large number of cases reviewable by the Competition Tribunal since the introduction of the *Competition Act*. Enforcement in recent years will be discussed later in this section.

In absolute terms, and relative to the U.S., the number of antitrust cases in Canada has been small. Prior to 1956, the number of prosecutions in combines cases averaged less than two per year. This number increased quite a bit in the 1970s, reaching 14.2 cases on average per year in the 1976–1980 period, and this increase is mainly due to the relatively large number of resale price maintenance cases during that period.

The number of antitrust prosecutions per year seems to have reached a peak in the 1984–1986 period. There is a noticeable decline in resale price maintenance cases after 1986, particularly in the 1990–91 period. This may reflect a growing reluctance on the part of the Bureau to pursue such cases in light of advances in the economic theory of resale price maintenance, or it might reflect the fact that the Bureau has had to devote a significant proportion of its resources to merger investigations since merger became a reviewable practice in 1986.

The results of recent enforcement practice for civil matters (matters reviewable by the Competition Tribunal other than mergers) and criminal matters are presented in Tables 4.2 and 4.3.[8] The number of criminal charges laid per year, given in Table 4.3, is consistent with the lower levels of prosecutions observed in 1990 and 1991 in Table 4.1. Regarding civil matters, Table 4.2 indicates that most inquiries regarding civil matters are discontinued or dealt with through alternative case resolution (which includes written undertakings, informal agreements to stop particular practices, and restitution).[9] Relatively few cases are resolved through applications to the Competition Tribunal. This reluctance to make applications to the Competition Tribunal is also reflected in merger enforcement statistics, and discussed further in Section IX.[10]

With respect to the Crown's success at obtaining convictions in competition cases, Gorecki and Stanbury (1979, 1984) have found that the conviction rate ranged between 63 percent in the 1889–1910 period to 92 percent in the 1947–1955 period and 1966–1970 period. The win rate dropped to 50 percent in the 1981–1983 period. The Bureau's recent success rate under various sections of the Act is discussed later in this chapter. Penalties for those found to be in violation of the *Competition Act* include fines, imprisonment, loss of tariff protection, prohibition orders, loss of patent protection, publicity, and divestiture in the case of merger. Fines have been the pre-

---

[8] Recent enforcement activity with respect to mergers was discussed in Chapter 2.

[9] See Stanbury (1998).

[10] Historical statistics on merger enforcement are discussed in more detail in Chapter 2.

Table 4.2
Examinations and Disposition of Civil Matters, 1995–2003

Year	Examinations Commenced	Inquiries in Progress at Year End	Inquiries Resolved by Alternative Case Resolution	Applications to the Competition Tribunal	Discontinuances
1995	21	10	2	3	na
1996	28	13	3	1	na
1997	31	16	4	0	na
1998	41	5	4	4	11
1999	28	8	3	0	6
2000	43	10	5	0	5
2001	43	11	3	1	6
2002	42	12	2	1	5
2003	29	5	2	1	5

Source: *Annual Reports of the Director of Investigation and Research,Competition Act, for the Years Ending March 31, 1995; March 31, 1996; March 31, 1997; March 31, 1998; Annual Reports of the Commissioner of Competition for the Years Ending March 31, 1999; March 31, 2000; March 31, 2001; March 31, 2002, and March 31, 2003.* Reproduced with the permission of the Minister of Public Works and Government Services, 2004.

Table 4.3
Examinations and Disposition of Criminal Matters, 1995–2003

Year	Examinations Commenced	Inquiries in Progress at Year End	Matters Referred to Attorney General	Matters where Charges Were Laid	Matters where Attorney General Declined to Proceed or Withdrew Charges
1995	53	31	7	3	0
1996	55	24	4	4	1
1997	46	29	0	1	0
1998	39	20	3	3	1
1999	49	26	7	6	0
2000	37	22	9	6	1
2001	57	24	8	8	0
2002	29	26	5	3	0
2003	59	33	4	4	0

Source: *Annual Reports of the Director of Investigation and Research, Competition Act, for the Years Ending March 31, 1995; March 31, 1996; March 31, 1997; March 31, 1998; Annual Reports of the Commissioner of Competition for the Years Ending March 31, 1999; March 31, 2000; March 31, 2001; March 31, 2002, and March 31, 2003.* Reproduced with the permission of the Minister of Public Works and Government Services, 2004.

ferred remedy, but for most of the history of competition policy in Canada, they have been generally regarded as too low to deter anti-competitive conduct.

Since 1976, the Commissioner has had the authority to make representations before regulatory bodies at both the federal and provincial level. The number of these interventions reached a peak in the period from 1981 to 1985, during which there were 16.4 interventions per year. In contrast, there were 6.8 interventions per year from 1991 to 1995, 11.4 per year from 1996 to 2000, and 9.0 per year from 2001 to 2003.[11] More detail on regulatory interventions is available in Stanbury (1998).

One aspect of the Competition Bureau's strategy in regards to enforcement of the *Competition Act* is the issuance of detailed enforcement guidelines. The first of these, the *Merger Enforcement Guidelines*, was published in March 1991, and is modelled to some extent on the U.S. Department of Justice's 1984 *Merger Guidelines. Price Discrimination Enforcement Guidelines* and *Predatory Pricing Enforcement Guidelines* were subsequently published in 1992, and *Enforcement Guidelines on the Abuse of Dominance Provisions* were published in 2001. As well, the Bureau has recently begun a practice of publishing guidelines regarding the application of the *Competition Act* to specific industries. Since 2000, the Bureau has published *The Merger Enforcement Guidelines as Applied to a Bank Merger, Intellectual Property Enforcement Guidelines, Draft Enforcement Guidelines on the Abuse of Dominance in the Airline Industry,* and *Draft Enforcement Guidelines: The Abuse of Dominance Provisions (Sections 78 and 79 of the Competition Act) as Applied to the Retail Grocery Industry.* To date, the Commissioner has not produced a set of vertical restraint guidelines. In what follows, the Commissioner's primary enforcement guidelines will be reviewed along with the relevant sections of the *Competition Act* to which they pertain.

---

[11] Figures from 1981 to 1995 are collected by Joseph Montiero, as cited in Stanbury (1998). Later figures are from the *Annual Reports of the Director of Investigation and Research,* 1996–1998 and the *Annual Reports of the Commissioner of Competition,* 1999–2003.

Chapter 4

III. CONSPIRACY AND BID RIGGING

Section 45 of the *Competition Act* is the conspiracy section:

> 45.(1) Every one who conspires, combines, agrees or arranges with another person
> (a) to limit unduly the facilities for transporting, producing, manufacturing, supplying, storing or dealing in any product,
> (b) to prevent, limit or lessen, unduly, the manufacture or production of a product or to enhance unreasonably the price thereof,
> (c) to prevent or lessen, unduly, competition in the production, manufacture, purchase, barter, sale, storage, rental, transportation or supply of a product, or in the price of insurance on persons or property, or
> (d) to otherwise restrain or injure competition unduly,
> is guilty of an indictable offence and liable to imprisonment for a term not exceeding five years or to a fine not exceeding ten million dollars or to both.

Several qualifications then follow: (1) it is not necessary to prove that the conspiracy would eliminate completely or virtually competition in the market or that it was intended to have that effect in order for a conspiracy to be in violation of section 45(1); (2) the court may infer the existence of a conspiracy from circumstantial evidence, with or without direct evidence of communication between the parties; (3) it is necessary to prove that the parties intended to enter into the conspiracy, but it is not necessary to prove that the parties intended that the conspiracy have an effect as set out in section 45(1). Section 45 also contains a list of acceptable defences that the accused might use if charged with conspiracy.

Section 46, relating to foreign directives, extends section 45 to international cartels by allowing for the application of the Act when the conspirators are not located or incorporated in Canada. In particular, section 46 prohibits corporations from implementing in Canada foreign instructions that have the purpose of giving effect to a conspiracy or agreement that would have violated section 45 were it entered into in Canada.

Section 47 prohibits bid rigging where bid rigging means

> (a) an agreement or arrangement between or among two or more persons

whereby one or more of those persons agrees or undertakes not to submit a bid in response to a call or request for bids or tenders, or

(b) the submission, in response to a call or request for bids or tenders, of bids or tenders that are arrived at by agreement or arrangement between or among two or more bidders or tenderers,

where the agreement or arrangement is not made known to the person calling for or requesting the bids or tenders at or before the time when any bid or tender is made by any person who is a party to the agreement or arrangement.

The Crown has been reasonably successful at obtaining convictions under the conspiracy section of the *Competition Act*. Chandler and Jackson (2000) report that from 1986 to April 2000, there were 52 prosecutions concluded under sections 45, 46 and 47: 32 under section 45, 4 under section 46, and 16 under section 47. Of these, there were 36 guilty pleas, 5 convictions, 8 acquittals and 3 discharged cases. Total fines under these sections over the period from 1986 to April 2000 were greater than 178 million dollars. Cases under these sections have involved a wide variety of industries, including driving schools, pharmacies, ambulances, feed additives, and fax paper. Much of the Bureau's recent activity has involved international cartels that are prosecuted in other countries as well. In the period from July 2000 to October 2001, investigations in several international conspiracy cases led to fines greater than 19 million dollars. Recent cases of international cartels or bid rigging have involved graphite electrodes, chemicals and food preservatives, and bidding to supply the concrete base for the Hibernia Oil platform.

For much of the history of the conspiracy provisions of Canadian competition law, there has been a concern among the courts, lawyers and economists regarding the meaning of the term "unduly," and when a lessening of competition is undue.[12] One Supreme Court of Canada case to address this issue is *R. v. Nova Scotia Pharmaceutical Society* (1992).[13] The Nova Scotia Pharmaceutical Society, Pharmacy Association of Nova Scotia, and a number of pharmacists had been charged with two counts of conspiracy to prevent or lessen competition unduly, contrary to section 32(1)(c) of the *Combines Investigation Act*. Both counts related to the sale and

---

[12] See Green (1990) and Stanbury (1991) for a discussion of the major Supreme Court of Canada cases that have attempted to interpret the word "unduly."

[13] *R.v. Nova Scotia Pharmaceutical Society*, [1992] 2 S.C.R. 606.

offering for sale of prescription drugs and pharmacists' dispensing services prior to June 16, 1986. Those charged then moved for an order quashing the indictment on the basis that sections 32(1)(c), 32(1.1) and 32(1.3) of the Act violated the Canadian Charter of Rights and Freedoms and were therefore invalid. The Nova Scotia Supreme Court, Trial Division had granted the motion and quashed the indictment, but the Appeal Division of the Nova Scotia Supreme Court allowed the Crown's appeal. The issues involved in the appeal were the vagueness arising from the use of the word unduly, and the *mens rea* (or intent) required by the offence. The Supreme Court dismissed the appeal and held that section 32(1)(c) does not violate the Charter. In concluding the analysis of the vagueness issue, Gauthier, J. stated

> In summary, I find that s.32(1)(c) of the Act and its companion interpretative provision s.32(1.1) do not violate s.7 of the Charter on grounds of vagueness. The word "unduly" as such carries a connotation of seriousness. Considering further that s.32(1)(c) of the Act is one of the oldest and most important parts of Canadian public policy in the economic field, and that it mandates a partial rule of reason inquiry into the seriousness of the competitive effects of the agreement, Parliament has sufficiently delineated the area of risk and the terms of debate to meet the constitutional standard. Moreover, the rest of the Act and the case law have outlined a process of examination of market structure and behaviour under s.32(1)(c) of the Act, thus making it even more precise.

Another issue that has been raised with respect to the conspiracy section has to do with its ability to deter tacit collusion or conscious parallelism (see Carlton and Perloff, 2004, Ch. 5). It is recognized that one cannot realistically prevent an oligopolist from making profit-maximizing decisions that take into account possible rival firm reactions, or from having an incentive to coordinate behaviour with rivals to reach the monopoly solution, and that tacitly collusive behaviour that follows from this incentive may be beyond the reach of section 45. While one might not wish to legislate against tacit collusion directly, one might wish to prohibit facilitating practices when they enhance firms' abilities to reach and maintain tacit agreements. Howard and Stanbury's (1990) list of facilitating practices includes most-favoured-customer clauses and meeting-competition clauses in purchase agreements, public speeches by corporate executives, advance announcement of prices, delivered pricing, the use of pricing manuals, and certain exclusionary practices.[14] They would amend the *Competition Act* to allow the Competition Tribunal to prohibit facilitating practices where the practices are avoidable, there is substantial evidence of non-competitive performance over a period of time, the social costs of the practices outweigh their benefits to society, and the non-competitive performance is reasonably attributable to or made worse by the use of the facilitating practices.

Finally, many strategic alliances into which firms may enter would cause no concern under the *Competition Act*. There are many types of alliances that firms may pursue, including acquisitions of minority investments in alliance partners and exchanges or trades of goods and services. In an attempt to clarify which types of alliances would violate the Act, the Bureau released the bulletin *Strategic Alliances Under the Competition Act* in 1995. This bulletin discusses potential violations of the conspiracy provisions of the Act, as well as other sections of the Act regarding abuse of dominance or the merger provisions. The discussion of the conspiracy provisions focuses on why certain types of agreements would violate the Act, and how the elements of section 45 would be applied.

IV. PRICE DISCRIMINATION

The *Price Discrimination Enforcement Guidelines*, issued by the Director of Investigation and Research, Bureau of Competition Policy, in 1992, deal with section 50(1)(a) of the *Competition Act*, which reads as follows:

> 50.(1) Every one engaged in a business who
> (a) is a party or privy to, or assists in, any sale that discriminates to his knowledge, directly or indirectly, against competitors of a purchase of articles from him in that any discount, rebate, allowance, price concession or other advantage is granted to the purchaser over and above any discount, rebate, allowance, price concession or other advantage that, at the time the articles are sold to the purchaser, is available to the competitors in respect of a sale of articles of like quality and quantity...is guilty of an indictable offence and liable to imprisonment for a term not exceeding two years.

---

[14] Delivered pricing is covered by sections 80 and 81 of the *Competition Act*.

(2) It is not an offence under paragraph (1)(a) to be a party or privy to, or assist in, any sale mentioned therein unless the discount, rebate, allowance, price concession or other advantage was granted as part of a practice of discriminating as described in that paragraph.

Section 50(1)(a) is one of the criminal law provisions of the *Competition Act*. There have only been three convictions under this provision between 1935 and May 2004, all of which occurred since 1984. The prosecutions were not contested, and they resulted in fines ranging from $15,000 to $50,000 being imposed by the courts.[15]

Two questions naturally arise. One is why have there been so few prosecutions of price discrimination? The second question is why did the Director (now Commissioner of Competition) find it necessary to issue guidelines for price discrimination in light of the low level of enforcement activity? With respect to the second question, the Director indicated in the *Guidelines* (p. 3) that the price discrimination provision of the Act "regularly generates many requests for advice and interpretation from the Bureau." Further, "Through issuing guidelines, the Director wishes to foster compliance with the law, while ensuring that the business community recognizes the legitimate scope which exists, within the law, for the adoption of innovative pricing practices and strategies."

With respect to the first question, the lack of enforcement activity of section 50(1)(a) is due at least partly to the wording of the section and the type of price discrimination that is prohibited.[16] First, section 50(1)(a) does not prohibit what is probably the most commonly observed type of price discrimination: third degree price discrimination by sellers to final customers.[17] In order to be in violation of section 50(1)(a), the purchasers of the product from the price discriminator must be in competition with one another. Hence, it will have to be established that the purchasers compete in the same relevant product and geographic market. (See Section VIII below for a discussion of market definition.)

---

[15] See p. 2 of the *Price Discrimination Enforcement Guidelines* issued by the Director. Reproduced with the permission of the Minister of Public Works and Government Services, 2004.

[16] For a detailed discussion of the price discrimination section of the *Competition Act*, see Trebilcock et al. (2002, pp. 352–372).

[17] See Carlton and Perloff (2004, Ch. 9) for a discussion of third degree price discrimination.

Section 50(1)(a) only applies to sales of "articles of like quality and quantity," where the Director interprets the word "like" to mean similar. There is no precise definition of these terms. The Director does not view "like quality" as posing a problem since most price discrimination questions deal with prices paid by competitors purchasing identical articles. The Director is not so sanguine about "like quantity," saying only that "In order to determine whether one quantity is 'like' another, the Director will generally consider industry practices in pricing the articles." The Director also notes that volume-based discounts, functional discounts (discounts granted to a purchaser in return for certain services provided by the purchaser), and exclusive dealing discounts (granted to a purchaser that agrees to deal exclusively in the seller's articles) will generally not raise questions under section 50(1)(a) as long as they are *available* to all competing purchasers. Also permitted will be a "buying group," an association of independent firms which combines the volume of members' purchases for the purpose of qualifying for volume-based price discounts (although certain conditions apply).

Finally, to commit an offence under section 50(1)(a), a seller must have "knowledge" of the discrimination and must be engaging in a "practice" (which in the Director's view is a systematic pattern of behaviour) of discrimination.

With all of the requirements of the price discrimination section, it is not surprising that so few cases have been brought to court. Given that price discrimination will often be efficiency enhancing (see Carlton and Perloff, 2004, Ch. 9), it is perhaps just as well. It is difficult to conceive of many instances where price discrimination will result in a substantial lessening of competition in a market. Oddly enough, however, section 50(1)(a) does not require the Commissioner to show that competition has been lessened by price discrimination.

In June 1999, the Commissioner of Competition requested an independent study of the provisions of the *Competition Act* dealing with anti-competitive pricing and their enforcement by the Bureau. The House of Commons Standing Committee on Industry, Science and Technology requested the report in anticipation of a review of the pricing provisions of the Competition Act. Professors VanDuzer and Paquet issued the report on October 22, 1999. In their review of the enforcement of the price discrimination section of the Act over the period 1994/95 to 1998/99, they found that there were 88 complaints of price discrimination during this period, but zero formal enforcement proceedings. Their recommendation is that price discrimination should not be a criminal offence, but should be subject to civil review by the Competition Tribunal.

VanDuzer and Paquet (1999, p. 25) note that the Competition Bureau has, in a 1995 discussion paper on possible amendments to the *Competition Act*, raised the question of whether the price discrimination section should be abolished. Abolition of the section was also endorsed by the Consultative Panel on amendments to the *Competition Act* in its 1996 Report. More recently, in a 2002 Report of the Standing Committee on Industry, Science and Technology, it is recommended that the Government of Canada repeal the price discrimination provisions of the Act and include these prohibitions under the abuse of dominance provision (section 79). In the Committee's view, the prohibition should govern all types of products, including articles and services, and all types of transactions, not just sales.

The *National Consultation on the Competition Act Final Report*, issued by the Public Policy Forum, was just released on April 8, 2004. It thus remains to be seen whether the *Competition Act* will be amended to make price discrimination a civilly reviewable practice.

V. PREDATORY PRICING

The *Predatory Pricing Enforcement Guidelines*, issued by the Director of Investigation and Research, Bureau of Competition Policy in 1992, deal with section 50(1)(c) of the *Competition Act*, which reads as follows:

> 50(1) Every one engaged in a business who...
> (c) engages in a policy of selling products at prices unreasonably low, having the effect or tendency of substantially lessening competition or eliminating a competitor, or designed to have that effect, is guilty of an indictable offence and liable to imprisonment for a term not exceeding two years.

Note that unlike price discrimination, in order for predatory pricing to be an offence under the Act, it must have "the effect or tendency of substantially lessening competition or eliminating a competitor, or designed to have that effect." Like price discrimination, there have been few predatory pricing cases. Up to the time that the Guidelines were issued, there had been two cases of record: *R. v. Hoffman - La Roche*

(1980) and *R. v. Consumers Glass Co.* (1981).[18] Between 1980 and 1990, the Director received some 550 complaints alleging an offence under the predatory pricing provisions. Of those, 23 resulted in formal inquiries under the Act, four were referred to the Attorney General, and three resulted in the laying of charges. With respect to the latter three cases, the accused was acquitted in one (*Consumers Glass*), and charges were withdrawn at the preliminary hearing in another.[19] Still it is not possible to infer from the enforcement record that predatory pricing is in fact rare. Rather, predatory pricing could be difficult to detect given the data available and the predatory pricing rules used by the Commissioner. If predatory pricing is rare, it could be because firms find other forms of predatory conduct more attractive.

Due to the paucity of cases, the Commissioner has not received a great deal of guidance with respect to the meaning of the phrase "selling products at prices unreasonably low." In *Hoffman - La Roche*, the Court stated that "if an article is sold for more than cost, it can never be held to be 'unreasonable.'" However, the Court refrained from adopting a particular predatory pricing rule, suggesting that price-cost comparisons would not be sufficient to establish a violation of section 50(1)(c). The Court in *Consumers Glass* took a similar approach. The Court found that the prices charged were between average variable and average total cost, but that the industry suffered from chronic over-capacity. Since the prices could be loss minimizing rather than predatory, the Court declined to convict Consumers Glass of predatory pricing.

The Director's enforcement guidelines were apparently influenced by these decisions. The Director stated that simple cost-based rules will not be adopted for evaluating allegations of predatory pricing. Rather, the context in which the alleged predation is occurring will be considered. The Director proposed using a two-stage approach to evaluate whether prices are unreasonably low, and this approach is similar to that proposed by Joskow and Klevorick (1981). The first stage analysis focuses on market

---

[18] See *R. v. Hoffman - La Roche* (1980), 28 O.R. (2d) 164; affirmed (1981), 33 O.R. (2d) 694 (C.A.) and *R. v. Consumers Glass Co.* (1981), 33 O.R. (2d) 228.

[19] See *Predatory Pricing Enforcement Guidelines*, p. 1. In a private action brought under section 36 of the *Competition Act*, Boehringer alleged that Bristol-Myers was selling its Taxol product at prices below its average total cost. Bristol-Myers filed a motion for summary judgment. The Court granted the application for summary judgment. The Court held that Bristol-Myers had not sold its drug below Boehringer's price, but was merely matching Boehringer's price. It further held that matching Boehringer's price was not unfair even if that price was below cost. See *Boehringer Ingelheim (Canada) Inc. v. Bristol-Myers Squibb Canada Inc.*, Ontario Court of Justice (General Division), October 9, 1998.

structure and market power, and is designed to determine whether the alleged predatory pricing could produce anti-competitive effects. The Guidelines state that the Director will examine market shares and concentration (and will therefore need to define relevant product and geographic markets using the criteria set out in the Director's *Merger Enforcement Guidelines* (1991)), and the conditions of entry, particularly whether the incumbent firm has a cost advantage relative to potential entrants and the extent to which entry or expansion into a market entails sunk costs.

If a firm is found in the first stage analysis to have market power, then the Commissioner will proceed to the second stage analysis of prices and costs. Here, a price set at or above the average total costs of the alleged predator will not be regarded as unreasonably low, regardless of the alleged predator's market power. A price set below average variable cost will be regarded as unreasonably low unless there is a clear justification. A price between average variable and average total cost may be unreasonably low, depending on the circumstances.

The price/cost test being proposed in the Guidelines is similar to the one proposed by Areeda and Turner (1975). The Areeda-Turner test focused on whether price was below "reasonably anticipated" short run marginal cost or average variable cost. Areeda and Turner did not permit a monopolist to defend below cost pricing on the grounds that its price was promotional or merely met an equally low price of a competitor.

The Competition Bureau has recently proposed changes to the *Predatory Pricing Enforcement Guidelines* that would recognize avoidable cost as the appropriate cost concept for the price/cost test Avoidable costs include variable costs and product-specific fixed costs that are not sunk. By focusing on avoidable costs, the Bureau will be able to apply the price/cost test to multiproduct firms where average total costs are not well defined and where the treatment of common costs becomes an issue.

Other important changes to the guidelines were also proposed in the draft "Enforcement Guidelines for Illegal Trade Practices: Unreasonably Low Pricing Policies," which were issued in March 2002. First, there was recognition that a reputation for predation can be an entry barrier created by predatory conduct. Second, there was recognition of the possibility that established firms might expand into a new market and engage in predatory behaviour against incumbent firms. As an example, a large supermarket chain could open a store or stores in an area where it previously did not operate. Given the chain's deep pockets, it may decide to adopt a low pricing policy in order to eliminate one or more established supermarkets. In determining whether the low pricing is a concern, the draft Guidelines (p.18) state that the Bureau will consider whether the pricing is promotional, "the length of the promotional period, the relative sizes of the price differences in relation to its other markets, whether and for how long the new entrant has achieved a foothold in the new market and the competitive conditions in the new market."

The Bureau will also consider whether the new entrant is operating its stores with revenues below avoidable costs, whether there is some reasonable alternative explanation for its conduct, whether the conduct would harm competition in the market, and whether the entrant's prices are lower than prices it charges elsewhere for the same products under similar competitive circumstances. The Bureau will also seek to determine whether the new entrant is more efficient than the incumbent firm.

The Competition Bureau received a number of comments on the draft guidelines, and hence the guidelines are undergoing further revision.

As with price discrimination, VanDuzer and Paquet (1999) examined the Competition Bureau's enforcement record with respect to predatory pricing over the period April 1994 to March 1999. During this period, the Bureau received 382 complaints alleging predatory pricing, but there were no formal enforcement proceedings. In terms of the disposition of the complaints, there was a failure to meet the requirements of the offence in 200 of them and insufficient information in 48.

VanDuzer and Paquet (1999, p. 74) believe that the requirement in section 50(1)(c) that the alleged predator be selling at prices that are unreasonably low is very vague, and that the existing case law does not provide a complete methodology for determining when prices are unreasonably low. They recommend (on p. 83) that predatory pricing should not be a criminal offence, but should be subject to civil review.

The Standing Committee on Industry, Science and Technology made a similar recommendation in its report on *A Plan to Modernize Canada's Competition Regime* (2002). The Committee recommended that section 50(1)(c) be repealed and that the *Competition Act* be amended to make predatory pricing an anti-competitive act within the civil abuse of dominance provision (section 79). While making predatory pricing subject to civil review would reduce the standard of proof that the Commissioner must meet to win a case, including predatory pricing in the abuse of dominance section would restrict predatory pricing cases to those situations where the requirements of section 79 can be met. These requirements will be discussed in the next section.

VI. ABUSE OF DOMINANT POSITION

Besides taking a predation case under section 50(1)(c), the Director has the option of pursuing certain types of predation cases under the abuse of dominant position provisions (sections 78–79) of the *Competition Act*. Abuse of dominant position is a practice reviewable by the Competition Tribunal, and includes the following (non-exhaustive set of) acts:

(a) squeezing, by a vertically integrated supplier, of the margin available to an unintegrated customer who competes with the supplier, for the purpose of impeding or preventing the customer's entry into, or expansion in, a market;

(b) acquisition by a supplier of a customer who would otherwise be available to a competitor of the supplier, or acquisition by a customer of a supplier who would otherwise be available to a competitor of the customer, for the purpose of impeding or preventing the competitor's entry into, or eliminating the competitor from, a market;

(c) freight equalization on the plant of a competitor for the purpose of impeding or preventing the competitor's entry into, or eliminating the competitor from, a market;

(d) use of fighting brands introduced selectively on a temporary basis to discipline or eliminate a competitor;

(e) pre-emption of scarce facilities or resources required by a competitor for the operation of a business, with the object of withholding the facilities or resources from a market;

(f) buying up of products to prevent the erosion of existing price levels;

(g) adoption of product specifications that are incompatible with products produced by any other person and are designed to prevent his entry into, or to eliminate him, from a market;

(h) requiring or inducing a supplier to sell only or primarily to certain customers, or to refrain from selling to a competitor, with the object of preventing a competitor's entry into, or expansion in, a market;

(i) selling articles at a price lower than the acquisition cost for the purpose of disciplining or eliminating a competitor;

(j) acts or conduct of a person operating a domestic service, as defined in subsection 55(1) of the *Canada Transportation Act*, that are specified under paragraph 2(a); and

(k) the denial by a person operating a domestic service, as defined in subsection 55(1) of the *Canada Transportation Act*, of access on reasonable commercial terms to facilities or services that are essential to the operation in a market of an air service, as defined in that subsection, or refusal by such person to supply such facilities or services on such terms.

Practices (c), (d) and (i) are forms of predatory conduct. The Competition Bureau, on page 24 of its *Enforcement Guidelines on the Abuse of Dominance Provisions*, released in July 2001, has provided a succinct interpretation of (c).

> In this form, predatory pricing occurs when a firm bases freight charges on the distance of a customer from the rival's plant, as opposed to the distance from the dominant firm's own plant. By using the rival's plant as a base point, the dominant firm(s) effectively earns a lower margin on customers located near its rival as compared to customers located near its own plant. This could amount to selective price cutting, that is, price cutting to buyers most likely to deal with the dominant firm's (firms') rival(s), with predatory intent.

Practice (d) involves something that might properly be called spatial predation. It is a strategy that can be carried out in a product market (e.g., ready-to-eat cereal), in which case the fighting brands are being introduced in a "characteristics space" (see Carlton and Perloff, 2004, Ch. 7). Alternatively, it is a strategy that can be employed in a geographic market, for example by retail firms. As one example, the Director of Investigation and Research argued in his analysis of the state of competition in the Canadian petroleum industry that vertically integrated companies like Imperial Oil and Shell had introduced second brand retail outlets in the late 1960s and early 1970s in an effort to restrain the pricing behaviour of independents.[20] The second brand outlets could be located in the neighbourhoods of price-cutting independents, and the second

---

[20] See Section H.5.c. of the Director of Investigation and Research (1981), *The State of Competition in the Canadian Petroleum Industry, Vol. VI, The Marketing of Gasoline.*

brand outlets' prices could be reduced while maintaining higher prices at the primary brand outlets.[21]

As a second example, Von Hohenbalken and West (1984) examined a hypothesis of locational predation using supermarket location data from Edmonton, Alberta. The choice of data to analyze was motivated by an anti-combines case involving Canada Safeway Ltd., a supermarket firm operating in western Canada. On October 11, 1972, the Attorney General of Canada laid an Information against Canada Safeway, charging that Canada Safeway was a party to a monopoly in the grocery retailing industry in the cities of Calgary and Edmonton between January 1, 1965, and October 10, 1972. On September 17, 1973, the Attorney General applied for and received, in the Supreme Court of Alberta, Orders of prohibition pursuant to section 30(2) of the *Combines Investigation Act*.[22] The Orders placed constraints on Safeway's expansion in Calgary and Edmonton for a period of five years, and prohibited localized price cutting and excessive advertising. While a predatory location strategy was not specifically mentioned among the activities charged or proscribed, Von Hohenbalken and West regarded the strategy as a plausible explanation for Safeway's apparent market dominance, and thus tested the following hypothesis:

> if an established retail firm has been a successful locational predator, then there exists evidence that (a) new stores of an entering firm are challenged by stores of the established firm built in their neighbourhood, (b) the predator's new plants are located so as to force losses on the entrant's plants, (c) the entrant ceases to construct new plants, (d) the entrant eventually withdraws from the market.

Using Edmonton supermarket location data for the years 1959 to 1973, the market areas of stores were calculated. Comparisons of average market areas of different firms' stores over time led to the conclusion that the data were consistent with Canada

---

[21] The Restrictive Trade Practices Commission, in its report on *Competition in the Canadian Petroleum Industry* (1986, p. 306), states that the second brands were developed by the vertically integrated petroleum companies in the 1960s to compete in the so-called discount-price segment of the gasoline market. While the integrated firms argued that the second brands were used to satisfy the price-conscious segment of market demand (and were therefore an instrument of retail price discrimination), the question remains as to whether they were also designed to deter the entry and expansion of the independents.

[22] *R. v. Canada Safeway Ltd.* (1973), 14 C.C.C. (2d) 14 (Alta. T.D.).

Safeway having engaged in locational predation against Loblaw, Dominion, and Tom Boy.[23] In a subsequent paper, Von Hohenbalken and West (1986) tested for whether Safeway's locational strategy was consistent with the creation of a reputation for predation that deterred future entry. Their analysis of Edmonton supermarket location data from 1959 to 1982 led them to conclude that the data were consistent with entry being deterred, which permitted Safeway to delay the costly opening of new supermarkets.

Anti-competitive act (i) describes a restrictive form of predatory pricing. For a firm to be engaged in this anti-competitive act, it must be shown that pricing was below acquisition cost, that it involved articles (not services), and that it was done for the purpose of disciplining or eliminating a competitor.[24] This anti-competitive act could be alleged in the case of a supermarket that was engaged in an extreme form of loss leading (selling many products at prices below their acquisition costs for example).[25]

Returning to the list of anti-competitive acts, (a), (b), (e), (f), (g), and (h) entail some form of market foreclosure that can have the effect of raising rivals' costs and deterring entry and expansion in a market.[26] The possibility of anti-competitive act (a) may have been of some concern among independent gasoline stations that acquired their gasoline from vertically integrated oil companies. The concern would be that the vertically integrated oil companies could raise the wholesale cost of gasoline to the independents while lowering the retail price at the vertically integrated companies' own gas stations. This type of vertical squeeze could reduce the margins of the independents to a point where it is no longer profitable to continue operating.

Anti-competitive acts (b), (f), and (h) are types of conduct that have been examined in

---

[23] For a more agnostic view regarding the notion of spatial predation and its reputation effect, see McFetridge (1990).

[24] In the *NutraSweet* case, the Director of Investigation and Research attempted to apply paragraph 78(i) to a manufacturer that was selling its product below its manufacturing cost. The Competition Tribunal rejected this argument. See *Canada (Director of Investigations and Research) v. NutraSweet Co.* [1990], 32 C.P.R. (3d), (Comp. Trib.).

[25] Concerns about possible anti-competitive behaviour in the Canadian grocery industry have prompted the Bureau to issue draft *Enforcement Guidelines: The Abuse of Dominance Provisions (Sections 78 and 79 of the Competition Act) as Applied to the Retail Grocery Industry*, December 17, 2001.

[26] For a discussion of the theory of raising rivals' costs, see Carlton and Perloff (2004, Ch. 11).

a raising rivals' cost context by Krattenmaker and Salop (1986). With respect to anti-competitive act (e), the Competition Bureau (2001a) has written the following:

> Alternatively, the dominant firm(s) may raise its rival's costs by pre-empting low cost inputs, forcing the rival to use higher cost inputs. Even if this strategy did not result in the exit of the rival, it could be profitable for the dominant firm if it resulted in the rival being a less effective competitor, allowing the dominant firm to increase its own prices. Preemption could also take the form of acquisition or control of the supply of a necessary input in production, such as production sites or facilities that are not easily replicated.

Anti-competitive acts (j) and (k) were added to section 78 of the *Competition Act* with the passage of Bill C-26, which came into force on July 5, 2000. These changes to the Act were motivated by the acquisition of Canadian Airlines by Air Canada, and the Government's belief that legislative changes were required in order to protect competition in the Canadian airline industry. Anti-competitive act (j) makes reference to paragraph (2)(a) of section 78. This paragraph allows the Governor in Council to make regulations specifying acts or conduct for the purpose of anti-competitive act (j), and facilities or services that are essential to the operation of an air service for the purpose of (k).

The Governor in Council subsequently passed "Regulations Respecting Anti-competitive Acts of Persons Operating a Domestic Service" (the "airline regulations") on August 23, 2000. These regulations set out eight anti-competitive acts, for purposes of paragraph 78(1)(j), relevant only for a person operating a domestic service (a domestic air carrier). Among the anti-competitive acts appearing in the airline regulations are (1) operating or increasing capacity on a route or routes at fares that do not cover the avoidable costs of providing the service, (2) preempting airport facilities, services, take-off or landing slots with the object of withholding the airport facilities, services or slots from the market, and (3) using a loyalty marketing program for the purpose of disciplining or eliminating a competitor or impeding or preventing a competitor's entry into, or expansion in, a market.[27]

The airline regulations also specify what are essential facilities or services for purposes

---

[27] A detailed discussion of the airline regulations appears in Eckert and West (2002).

of paragraph 78(1)(k). These are facilities or services

(a) that are required in order to provide a competitive air service;
(b) that cannot reasonably or practicably be purchased, acquired, provided or replicated by another air carrier on its own behalf;
(c) that are effectively controlled by the air carrier who denies access to them or refuses supply of them; and
(d) that can be feasibly provided to another air carrier, having regard to operational or safety considerations, or legitimate business justifications of the air carrier referred to in paragraph (c).

The airline regulations go on to provide a list of facilities or services that may be essential.[28] Anti-competitive act (k), along with the specification of what constitutes an essential facility or service, are similar to what has become known as the "essential facilities doctrine" in the U.S. However, the essential facilities doctrine in the U.S. would not be restricted in application to the airline industry (see Carlton and Perloff, 2004, Ch. 19).

To find that there has been an abuse of dominant position, section 79(1) states that the Competition Tribunal must find, on application by the Commissioner, that

(a) one or more persons substantially or completely control, throughout Canada or any area thereof, a class or species of business,
(b) that person or those persons have engaged in or are engaging in a practice of anti-competitive acts, and
(c) the practice has had, is having or is likely to have the effect of preventing or lessening competition substantially in a market.

The Tribunal may then make an order prohibiting all or any of those persons from engaging in that practice. If that is not sufficient to restore competition in the market, the Tribunal may make an order which requires persons to take such actions, including the divestiture of assets or shares, as are reasonable and necessary to overcome the effects of the anti-competitive practice in the market. Before finding that a practice has

---

[28] The Competition Bureau issued draft *Enforcement Guidelines on the Abuse of Dominance in the Airline Industry* in February 2001. The guidelines can be found on the Competition Bureau's website at www.competition.ic.gc.ca.

had, is having, or is likely to have the effect of substantially preventing or lessening competition, the Tribunal is instructed under section 79(4) to consider whether the practice is a result of "superior competitive performance." Note that the phrase superior competitive performance does not necessarily have the same meaning as economic efficiency. Note also that the Tribunal is merely instructed to "consider" whether the practice is a result of superior competitive performance, without placing any weight on this consideration in the Tribunal's decision.

The *Competition Act* was further amended on June 21, 2002. The Act was amended to allow the Commissioner, in the case of an alleged abuse of dominance in the airline industry, to extend a temporary order beyond the 80-day maximum until the Commissioner has had sufficient time to receive and review information required to determine whether to make an application before the Tribunal. The Act was also amended to allow the Tribunal to impose administrative monetary penalties of up to $15 million when, after a hearing, it finds that an air carrier has abused its dominant market position.[29]

The Competition Bureau (2001a) has discussed the Tribunal's interpretation of the elements that must be satisfied for the Tribunal to find an abuse of dominance in a given case. Element (a) has been interpreted to mean that one must show that a firm has market power in some relevant product and geographic market. The interpretation of element (b) has focused on the word "practice." According to the Competition Bureau (2001a, p. 2), a practice can be one occurrence that is sustained or systematic over a period of time, or a number of different acts taken together that have the effect of substantially preventing or lessening competition. The Bureau (p. 3) also notes that the meaning of element (c) has been established in case law. "The question is whether the anti-competitive acts engaged in by a firm or group of firms serve to preserve, entrench or enhance their market power."

Between the time the *Competition Act* was passed in 1986 and 2001, there were four Tribunal decisions that involved contested applications. Two other cases involved joint abuse and were resolved by way of Tribunal consent orders. The first case to be brought under section 79 was filed in 1989; the decision in *Director of Investigation*

---

[29] See the Competition Bureau's press release, "Amendments with Respect to the Airline Industry," available on the Competition Bureau's website at http://competition.ic.gc.ca/epic/internet/incb-bc.nsf/en/ct02390e.html.

and Research v. The NutraSweet Company was rendered in 1990.[30] This case concerned the contractual and pricing practices of NutraSweet Canada, which held the Canadian use patent for aspartame (a high-intensity sweetener largely used in diet soft drinks) until July 1987. Worldwide sales of aspartame in 1989 were approximately 7500 metric tonnes, 75 percent of which were sold in the U.S., 5 percent in Canada, and 15 percent in Europe. NutraSweet accounted for all sales of aspartame in the U.S. in 1989 because its patent did not expire there until December 1992, while it held over 95 percent and 80 percent of Canadian and European sales, respectively. NutraSweet sold 359 tonnes of aspartame in Canada in 1989, and five soft drink franchisers accounted for over 300 tonnes. The Director's investigation of NutraSweet was initiated by a complaint made by Tosoh, a Japanese corporation attempting to expand its sales of aspartame in Canada.

The Director identified eight anti-competitive acts allegedly practiced by NutraSweet, four of which relate to the terms of NutraSweet's supply contracts, and were allegedly used to induce Canadian aspartame buyers to deal exclusively with NutraSweet. Below cost pricing was also alleged. The Competition Tribunal found that NutraSweet had engaged in a practice of anti-competitive acts that lessened competition substantially under section 79, including use in its supply contracts of exclusive supply and use clauses, logo display allowances, cooperative marketing allowances, meet-or-release clauses, most-favoured nation clauses, and the use of its U.S. patent to foreclose competition by a system of rebates on exports from the U.S. to induce Canadian importers to have only NutraSweet aspartame used in products purchased by them in Canada. The Tribunal also concluded that NutraSweet had violated section 77 in that NutraSweet had lessened competition substantially by inducing exclusive dealing with its aspartame customers through its financial incentives or fidelity rebates, and its exclusivity clauses.

In reaching its conclusion, the Tribunal chose to define the product market as aspartame, rejecting market definitions that would have included caloric sweeteners or other high-intensity sweeteners. The Tribunal chose to define the geographic market as Canada, rejecting NutraSweet's position that the market was worldwide. The Tribunal accepted the argument that there were very serious barriers to entry of new manufacturers of aspartame because of the patent portfolios of existing producers, significant economies of scale relative to existing world demand for aspartame, and

---

[30] See *Canada (Director of Investigation and Research) v. NutraSweet Co.*, *supra* at note 24.

sunk costs that increased the risks of entry. The Tribunal rejected NutraSweet's position that there were numerous potential entrants represented by general fine chemical firms or former aspartame producers. The Tribunal also rejected NutraSweet's submission that it could not exploit market power since its largest customers, Coke and Pepsi, were capable of producing aspartame to satisfy their own demand. The *NutraSweet* case nicely illustrates how different the positions of the Director and respondent can be with respect to market definition, entry barriers, and market power, all of which are critical factors in the Tribunal's ultimate decision.

The second Tribunal decision in an abuse case was rendered in 1992, and has become known as the *Laidlaw* case.[31] This case concerned the acquisition and contractual practices of Laidlaw Waste Systems Ltd. Laidlaw provided lift-on-board garbage collection and disposal service, largely for commercial enterprises such as restaurants and office buildings. The relevant geographic markets covered by the case were determined by the Tribunal to consist of the Courtney-Comox-Cumberland area of British Columbia and the Campbell River area of British Columbia, both located on Vancouver Island. The Director applied for orders, pursuant to section 79 of the *Competition Act*, prohibiting Laidlaw from engaging in certain anti-competitive acts, including a pattern of acquisitions allegedly designed to create and maintain a monopoly position together with contracting practices designed to preserve that position.

The Tribunal accepted that the pattern of acquisitions was for the purpose of initially acquiring a monopolistic position in the markets in question and then eliminating competitors from those markets. This conclusion was buttressed by the restrictive covenants in the acquisition agreements which prevented the owner of the acquired firm from setting up a similar business within a 300-mile radius of the purchased business.

The Tribunal also found that there was no reason for any of the provisions of Laidlaw's contracts with its customers other than to create barriers to entry by making customers' purchase decisions inflexible. For example, the contracts had three-year terms, automatic roll-over provisions (i.e., renewal unless the customer refused renewal in advance and in writing), liquidated damages clause, and exclusivity provision which

---

[31] See *Canada (Director of Investigation and Research) v. Laidlaw Waste Systems Ltd.* [1992], 40 C.P.R. (3d) 289 (Comp. Trib.).

were judged to bind the customer to Laidlaw for a long period of time. The contracts also had negative option price clauses (meaning that Laidlaw's price increases were assumed to be acceptable to the customer unless the customer formally objected) and right of first refusal and right to compete clauses. The Tribunal found that the entry barriers created by Laidlaw's contracts together with its acquisition practices resulted in a substantial lessening of competition, while its market share and pricing practices suggested that it was a dominant firm with market power. The Tribunal therefore issued orders (a) prohibiting Laidlaw from acquiring any competitor in the market for a period of three years, and (b) altering terms of its existing contracts.

The *Laidlaw* and *NutraSweet* cases are similar in that they both deal with firms that used provisions in their contracts with their customers to assist them in deterring entry into their markets. They also show that the Tribunal will consider practices other than those listed in section 78, including merger, as possible abuses of dominant position.

In a third abuse case, *Director of Investigation and Research v. D&B Companies of Canada Ltd.* (usually referred to as the *Nielsen* case), the Director challenged Nielsen's system of exclusive contracts.[32] According to Draper and West (1999–2000), Nielsen paid grocers and related retailers for data collected from cash register scanning equipment. These data were then processed and sold as sales data and analysis to product manufacturers for use in marketing programs. Nielsen was the sole purchaser of the scanner data, and the sole supplier of the processed sales data to manufacturers. Under the long-term contracts used by Nielsen, retailers would supply scanner data exclusively to Nielsen. Long-term contracts with incentives for exclusivity were also used with the purchasers of sales data. Contracts were staggered and came up for renewal at different times.

The Director argued that the vertical restraints of the exclusive contracts used by Nielsen constituted market foreclosure of horizontal competitors, because they created barriers to entry. A potential competitor would be unable to attract sufficient customers to make entry profitable, since manufacturers valued the completeness of the Nielsen data, which covered sales by all major retailers. The Director contended that Nielsen introduced the system of contracts for the purpose of market foreclosure.

---

[32] See *Canada (Director of Investigation and Research) v. The D&B Companies of Canada Ltd.* [1995], 64 C.P.R. (3d) 216 (Comp. Trib.).

After analyzing the evidence presented by both parties, the behaviour of potential competitors, and Canadian market conditions relative to those in other countries, the Tribunal concluded that the system of exclusive contracts used by Nielsen did foreclose competition and represented an abuse of dominance. Nielsen was prohibited from enforcing the exclusivity portions of contracts with retailers, and exclusivity terms in contracts with purchasers were eliminated.

The fourth abuse of dominance case prior to 2001 involving a contested application for which there is a Tribunal decision is the *Tele-Direct* (1997) case.[33] The two cases for which Tribunal consent orders were issued prior to 2001 are the *Interac* (1996) and *CANYPS* (1994) cases.[34] Discussions of these cases can be found in Competition Bureau (2001a) and Trebilcock et al. (2002, Ch. 8). More recently, the *Commissioner of Competition v. Enbridge Services Inc.*, for which an application was filed in December 2001, was settled by a Tribunal consent order.[35] The case of *Commissioner of Competition v. Canada Pipe Co.*, for which an application was filed in October 2002, is still ongoing.[36]

Another ongoing abuse of dominance case is the *Commissioner of Competition v. Air Canada*. The Commissioner filed a notice of application in this case on March 5, 2001. The application, according to the Competition Tribunal, states that between April 1, 2000 and March 5, 2001, Air Canada responded to the entry of WestJet Airlines Ltd. and CanJet Airlines on seven central and Atlantic Canada routes by increasing its capacity and/or decreasing its fares in a manner that did not cover the avoidable cost of operating the flights on the route, in violation of paragraphs 1(a) and 1(b) of the airline regulations.[37] This case is unusual in that, at the request of the Commissioner and Air Canada, the Competition Tribunal ordered that the application

---

[33] *Director of Investigation and Research v. Tele-Direct (Publications) Inc.* (1997), 73 C.P.R. (3d) 1 (Comp. Trib.).

[34] *Canada (Director of Investigation and Research) v. Bank of Montreal et al.* (1996), 68 C.P.R. (3d) 527 (Comp. Trib.); *Director of Investigation and Research v. AGT Directory Limited* (18 November 1994), CT9402/19, Consent Order, [1994] C.C.T.D. no. 24 (QL).

[35] *The Commissioner of Competition v. Enbridge Services Inc.*, CT-01/008 [2002] C.C.T.D. No.8.

[36] Competition Tribunal decisions can be obtained from the Competition Tribunal's website at www.ct-tc.gc.ca. Reproduced with the permission of the Minister of Public Works and Government Services, 2004.

[37] See *Commissioner of Competition v. Air Canada*, 2003 Comp. Trib. 13, paragraph 1.

be heard in two phases. Phase I was to deal with the application of the avoidable cost test to two sample routes over the relevant time period, while Phase II was to deal with the balance of the application (e.g., whether there was a practice of anti-competitive acts that resulted in a substantial lessening or prevention of competition).

During Phase I, the Competition Tribunal was to decide the appropriate unit or units of capacity to examine for the avoidable cost test, what categories of costs are avoidable and when they become avoidable, the appropriate time period or periods to examine, and what, if any, recognition should be given to beyond contribution.[38] The Tribunal was also to decide whether Air Canada had operated or increased capacity on the Toronto/Moncton and Halifax/Montreal routes at fares that did not cover the avoidable costs of providing the service.

The Tribunal issued its decision in Phase I on July 22, 2003. The Tribunal decided that the appropriate unit of capacity is the schedule flight, that the avoidable costs are avoidable from the outset by virtue of shedding, redeployment or disposal, that the appropriate time period to examine is one month, and that no recognition should be given to beyond contribution. On this basis, the Tribunal also found that Air Canada had operated or increased capacity at fares that did not cover the avoidable costs of providing the service on the two routes examined over the time period covered by the application. It remains to be seen whether the balance of the application will be heard and whether Air Canada will be found to have engaged in an abuse of dominant position under section 79 of the *Competition Act*.

The *Air Canada* case is important in that the Phase I decision is the first judicial interpretation in Canada of avoidable costs and how it might be determined whether a firm is operating with revenues that do not cover avoidable costs. As such, the decision might provide some guidance for future predation cases that attempt to implement a price/cost test based on an avoidable cost standard.

---

[38] Beyond contribution is the difference between beyond revenue and beyond cost, where beyond revenue consists of the prorated portions of the fares of through and connecting passengers that are allocated to the other flight segments of the trips of through and connecting passengers.

Chapter 4

VII. THE MERGER PROVISIONS OF THE *COMPETITION ACT*

Section 91 of the *Competition Act* defines a merger as "the acquisition or establishment, direct or indirect, by one or more persons, whether by purchase or lease of shares or assets, by amalgamation or by combination or otherwise, of control over or significant interest in the whole or a part of a business of a competitor, supplier, customer or other person." Section 92 states that "where, on application by the Commissioner, the Tribunal finds that a merger or proposed merger prevents or lessens, or is likely to prevent or lessen, competition substantially," the Tribunal may (a) in the case of a completed merger, order the merger to be dissolved, or parties to the merger to dispose of assets or shares, or (b) in the case of a proposed merger, order the parties not to proceed with the merger, in whole or in part.

Section 92(2) of the Act instructs the Tribunal not to find that a merger or proposed merger prevents or lessens competition substantially solely on the basis of evidence of concentration or market share. Section 93 provides a non-exhaustive set of criteria that the Tribunal may have regard to in determining whether a merger or proposed merger prevents or lessens or is likely to prevent or lessen competition substantially:

(a) the extent to which foreign products or competitors provide effective competition to the parties to a merger,
(b) whether a party to the merger has failed or is likely to fail,
(c) the availability of substitutes for products supplied by the merging firms,
(d) barriers to entry, including tariff and non-tariff barriers to international trade, interprovincial barriers to trade, and regulatory control over entry,
(e) the extent of effective competition remaining after the merger,
(f) whether the merger would result in the removal of a vigorous and effective competitor,
(g) the nature and extent of change and innovation in a relevant market.

Furthermore, under section 96 of the Act, the Tribunal is instructed not to make an order to dissolve or prohibit a merger if it finds that the merger is likely to bring about efficiency gains that will be greater than and will offset the effects of any prevention or lessening of competition that will result or likely result from the merger, and if such efficiency gains would not likely be attained were the merger dissolved or prohibited. Thus, the Tribunal may undertake a Williamson (1968) type of trade-off analysis. Section 96 specifies that in considering potential efficiency gains, the Tribunal should

110

consider the effect of such gains on increases in the real value of exports and whether the gains will lead to a significant substitution of domestic products for imported products. Finally, under section 96, the Tribunal must not conclude that a merger results in efficiency gains only because of a redistribution of income.

The Commissioner has three years from the date at which a merger is substantially complete to apply to the Tribunal for an order to dissolve or prohibit the merger. However, if the Commissioner has issued an advance ruling certificate to the merging firms indicating that there are insufficient grounds for the Commissioner to oppose the merger, then the Commissioner may not later apply to the Tribunal for an order under section 92 unless the Commissioner's opposition to the merger is based on new information.

Part IX of the *Competition Act* deals with "Notifiable Transactions." If the parties to a merger have assets or gross revenues from sales in excess of four hundred million dollars, or if the business being acquired has assets or gross revenues from sales in excess of thirty-five million dollars, then the parties to the merger must notify the Commissioner that the transaction is proposed and supply the Commissioner with information in accordance with part IX of the Act. A proposed transaction shall not be completed before the expiration of fourteen or forty-two days after the day on which the required information is provided to the Commissioner, depending upon the nature of the information required. Failure to notify is a criminal offence under section 65(2) and is subject to a fine of up to $50,000.

In practice, the Commissioner's review of large mergers will take longer than forty-two days. The parties will usually refrain from completing a merger until the Commissioner's review is complete. This is especially true if the parties are involved in negotiations with the Commissioner over the terms of the proposed merger.

For particular industries, the power to approve a merger may lie with other government ministries. Section 94 of the Act specifies that the Tribunal may not make an order dissolving or prohibiting a merger or ordering the divestiture of certain assets if (a) the transaction falls under the *Bank Act*, the *Cooperative Credit Associations Act*, the *Insurance Companies Act* or the *Trust and Loan Companies Act*, and is certified by the Minister of Finance as being in the public interest, or (b) the transaction is approved under the *Transportation Act* and certified to the Commissioner by the Minister of Transport. For transactions falling under the jurisdiction of the *Bank Act*, the *Transportation Act,* or other relevant acts, the relevant Minister may nonetheless request the opinion of the Commissioner before making a decision.

VIII. THE *MERGER ENFORCEMENT GUIDELINES*

In 1991, the Bureau of Competition Policy (now the Competition Bureau) released guidelines regarding how the merger provisions of the *Competition Act* would be enforced. Subsequent amendments to the merger provisions, and a particular decision by the Federal Court of Appeals, have rendered certain sections of the guidelines no longer relevant. A draft of revised merger enforcement guidelines was released in March 2004 for comments, but have not to date been adopted as policy. The main revisions suggested in the revised guidelines will be discussed at the end of this section.[39]

The Bureau will begin its analysis of a proposed merger by defining the relevant product and geographic markets within which the firms compete. The Bureau's principal market definition criterion is similar to the one that appears in the U.S. Department of Justice's *Merger Guidelines*, and focuses on a hypothetical monopolist test (Director of Investigation and Research, 1991, page 7):

> Conceptually, a relevant market for merger analysis under the Act is defined in terms of the smallest group of producers and smallest geographic area in relation to which sellers, if acting as a single firm (a 'hypothetical monopolist') that was the only seller of those products in that area, could profitably impose and sustain a significant and nontransitory price increase above levels that would likely exist in the absence of the merger.

The Bureau in most cases will consider a five percent price increase to be significant, and a one-year period to be nontransitory.

---

[39] In addition, the Bureau occasionally releases documents illustrating the application of guidelines to specific sectors. In 2003, the Bureau released the document *Merger Enforcement Guidelines as Applied to a Bank Merger*, which addresses how the methodology discussed in the merger guidelines would be used in the financial sector.

To apply this criterion to define a relevant product or geographic market, the Bureau will start with one of the merging parties and ask what would happen if it raised price by five percent for one year. If the price increase would not be sustainable because consumers would switch to substitute products, then the Bureau will take the firm producing the closest substitute to the merging firms' product, hypothetically merge the firms together and ask whether a five percent price increase can be sustained for a year. If it can, then that would be defined as the relevant product or geographic market. If the price increase would not be sustainable, the Bureau will repeat the exercise until the hypothetically merged firms can sustain a price increase.

Stigler and Sherwin (1985) have criticized this method of defining the relevant market as being nonoperational. Certainly given the data requirements it will often be difficult to apply the definition in a rigorous fashion. Perhaps for this reason, the Bureau has constructed a list of "evaluative criteria" that it will use to assess the extent of substitutability of products on the demand and supply side. Products that are close substitutes will be regarded as in the same market.

In defining the relevant product market, the Bureau will consider (a) views, strategies, behaviour and identity of buyers, (b) trade views, strategies and behaviour, (c) end use, (d) physical and technical characteristics, (e) switching costs, (f) price relationships and relative price levels (i.e. correlations of price movements), (g) cost of adapting or constructing production processes, distribution and marketing, and (h) existence of second hand, reconditioned, or leased products. In defining the relevant geographic market, the Bureau will consider (a) views, strategies, behaviour and identity of buyers, (b) trade views, strategies and behaviour, (c) switching costs, (d) transportation costs, (e) local set-up costs, (f) particular characteristics of the product, (g) price relationships and relative price levels, (h) shipment patterns, and (i) foreign competition.[40] A subset of these criteria will be applicable in each merger case. They can yield quite different conclusions regarding the nature and extent of competition in

---

[40] See Crampton (1991) for a discussion of how the Bureau has conducted its market definition analysis in certain merger cases. Crampton states that the Bureau had seldom found it necessary to undertake a formal "hypothetical monopolist" market definition analysis because "mergers that have been considered to have had sufficiently serious potential implications to warrant the preparation of a detailed assessment document have been of the variety that raised concerns about dominant firm behaviour, i.e., the unilateral exercise of market power, and have involved very thin markets where the identity of actual and potential competitors has been readily ascertainable."

the market when applied by the Commissioner, the Tribunal, and the parties to a merger. This in turn will have repercussions for the calculation of market shares and measures of concentration.

The Commissioner will use market share and concentration criteria to identify mergers that are unlikely to have anti-competitive consequences. In particular, the Commissioner generally will not challenge a merger on the basis of the merged firm's market power when the merged firm would have a market share of less than 35 percent. The Commissioner generally will not challenge a merger on the basis of an enhanced interdependent exercise of market power by two or more firms in the market when (a) the post-merger market share of the four largest firms in the market would be less than 65 percent, or (b) the post-merger market share of the merged firm would be less than 10 percent.[41]

If a merger exceeds the thresholds, the Bureau will have to undertake a more detailed analysis of the competitive effects of the merger, in part by considering the factors listed in section 93 (e.g., extent of foreign competition, possibility of a failing firm, entry barriers).

With respect to the failing firm defence of a merger, the Bureau will assess whether acquisition of the failing firm by a third party, retrenchment by the failing firm, or liquidation would likely result in a higher level of competition in the market than if the merger proceeded. The absence of such an alternative to the merger is regarded as sufficient to warrant a conclusion that a merger is not likely to prevent or lessen competition substantially.

In considering whether barriers to entry are significant factors in the relevant market of the merging firms, the Bureau will look at whether entry is likely to be delayed or hindered by the presence of absolute cost differences or the extent to which

---

[41] The Bureau will include in its calculation of the size of the market the entire actual output or capacity of firms located in the relevant market. However, where firms ship a significant proportion of their output outside the relevant market, and where this output could not be diverted back to the relevant market in the event of a five percent increase in price, the Bureau will exclude this output or associated capacity from the definition of the relevant market. In the case of output shipped into the relevant market by distant sellers, only the actual output sold in the relevant market will be included in the Bureau's calculation of market size.

investments cannot be recovered if entry is unsuccessful (i.e., the extent to which entry costs are sunk). The Commissioner will generally conclude that a merger is not likely to lessen competition substantially if as a result of the merger, sufficient entry occurs to ensure that a significant price increase is not sustainable in a substantial part of the relevant market for more than two years.

With respect to effective competition remaining, where it is clear that the level of effective competition remaining in the market is not likely to be reduced as a result of the merger, this alone will generally justify a conclusion by the Bureau not to challenge the merger.

The Bureau has added two other factors to the list in section 93 that it will consider in evaluating proposed mergers. The first is "market transparency" or the extent to which information is readily available in the market about competitors' prices, service, product quality and variety, advertising, etc. In the Bureau's view, as the level of transparency decreases, coordinated behaviour becomes increasingly difficult. Market transparency can be enhanced by a variety of facilitating practices, and evidence of these occurring in a relevant market would give the Bureau concern regarding possible anti-competitive effects of the merger. The second factor is "transaction value and frequency." As the frequency of sales of the relevant product decrease and as the value of each sale increases, interdependent behaviour is thought to be increasingly difficult.

A vertical merger generally will raise concern only if it increases barriers to entry at one of the stages of production (by necessitating entry at another stage of production) and enhances the firm's ability to exercise market power, or if upstream interdependence is facilitated because of enhanced monitoring of the upstream rival's price made possible by forward integration into retailing. A conglomerate merger will generally raise concerns only if it can be demonstrated that in the absence of the merger one of the merging firms would likely have entered the market de novo.

Part 5 of the *Merger Enforcement Guidelines* deals with the efficiency defence of a merger. Section 96 of the *Competition Act* instructs the Tribunal not to make an order under section 92 if it finds that a merger brings about efficiency gains that will be greater than and will offset the effects of any lessening of competition, and that the efficiency gains would not be obtained in the absence of the merger. The *Guidelines* discuss the efficiency gains that the Bureau would consider, and the determination of whether the efficiency gains "offset" the anti-competitive effects. However, the Bureau

115

has recently indicated on its website that "in light of the decision of the Federal Court of Appeal in the *Commissioner of Competition v. Superior Propane Inc.*, the Efficiency Exception Part 5 of the guidelines no longer applies."[42] This case is discussed in the following section.

On March 25, 2004, the Bureau released revised merger enforcement guidelines for public comment. The revised guidelines maintain the hypothetical monopolist test, market concentration thresholds, and other basic criteria discussed in the original guidelines. Most changes provide additional information regarding the Bureau's methodology. For example, the revised guidelines provide more detail regarding the definition of relevant product and geographic markets and expand the discussion of anti-competitive effects (including an extended discussion of the analysis of co-ordinated behaviour). In addition, the draft guidelines revise the discussion of the efficiencies defence. These guidelines will likely be revised again in response to comments received.

IX. ENFORCEMENT OF THE MERGER PROVISIONS OF THE *COMPETITION ACT*

Between June 1986 and June 1991, nine applications involving merger cases were made to the Competition Tribunal. According to Stanbury (1992, p. 427), four of the applications were for an order dissolving a merger pursuant to section 92 (one of these was delayed by a constitutional challenge which failed in July 1992 [*Couture/Sanimal*] and one resulted in a negotiated settlement approved by the Tribunal in the form of a consent order [*Air Canada/CAIL(Gemini)*]).[43] Three applications were for a consent order pursuant to section 105 (one was denied [*Palm Dairies*] while two were granted [*ABB/Westinghouse* and *Imperial Oil/Texaco*]).[44] Two applications were for an interim order to stop the closing of a merger (one resulted in a pre-closing restructuring [*Hostess/Frito Lay*] while the acquirer dropped the initial bid in the other case [*Institut Merieux*]).

---

[42] See http://competition.ic.gc.ca/epic/internet/incb-bc.nsf/en/ct01026e.html.

[43] *R. v. Alex Couture Inc.* (1990), 69 D.L.R. (4th) 635; *Canada (Director of Investigation and Research) v. Air Canada,* (Reasons for Consent Order) (1989), 27 C.P.R. (3d) 476 (Comp. Trib.).

[44] *Canada (Director of Investigation and Research) v. Palm Dairies Ltd.* (1986), 12 C.P.R. (3d) 540; *Canada (Director of Investigation and Research) v. Asea Brown Boveri Inc.* (1989), (Reasons for Consent Order) (CT-89/1, #1019a) (September 1989); *Canada (Director of Investigation and Research) v. Imperial Oil Ltd.,* 26 January 1990, Doc. No. CT-89/3 (Comp. Trib.) (unreported).

According to the Competition Bureau's annual reports, there have been 30 applications to the Tribunal regarding merger cases between June 1992 and June 2002, involving both consent agreements and contested cases. In contrast, over the same period, 23 cases were resolved without Tribunal involvement through restructuring (both pre-closing and post-closing) and undertakings (agreements between the Commissioner and the parties).

One of the reasons for reluctance to seek consent orders from the Tribunal is the difficulty that the Director has had in obtaining such orders. According to Stanbury (1992), the Tribunal had some difficulty deciding how much evidence it needed to hear and what role it should play in consent order proceedings. It refused to grant a consent order in *Palm Dairies* (1986), but then granted consent orders in *Gemini* (1989) and *ABB/Westinghouse* (1989). In *Imperial Oil/Texaco*, the Tribunal refused to grant the Director's application for a consent order without changing it to satisfy the Tribunal's concerns. Most recently, the Competition Tribunal in 2000 dismissed an application by the Commissioner for a consent order regarding the acquisition of a wholesale gasoline supply terminal and wholesale supply business in Ottawa by Ultramar Inc., a regional oil refiner. Because of the potential costs involved in delaying mergers on account of protracted consent order or contested merger proceedings before the Competition Tribunal, parties to a merger are anxious to negotiate with the Commissioner and agree to undertakings if they can keep the merger from coming before the Tribunal.

Trebilcock et al. (2002) report that by early 2001, the Competition Tribunal had provided decisions and adjudicated four contested merger proceedings. The Director lost the first contested merger application to the Tribunal since the 1986 Competition Act was passed on March 9, 1992. The Director had applied for an order directing Hillsdown (Canada) Ltd. to divest itself of the business operated by Ontario Rendering Company Ltd. (Orenco).[45] Hillsdown obtained control of Orenco when it acquired 50 percent of the common shares of Canada Packers Inc. in July 1990. The Tribunal denied the Director's application on the grounds that there was insufficient evidence that the merger resulted in a substantial lessening of competition and that the proposed divestiture would be ineffective at preserving competition in the market.[46]

---

[45] See *Canada (Director of Investigation and Research) v. Hillsdown Holdings (Canada Ltd.)* (1992), 41 C.P.R. (3d) 289.

[46] See Blakney (1992a) for a detailed summary of the Tribunal's decision in *Hillsdown*.

In a second contested merger, the Tribunal issued its decision on June 2, 1992, regarding the Director's application for divestiture orders against Southam Inc. in relation to its acquisition of two community newspapers and a real estate publication: the *Vancouver Courier*, the *North Shore News*, and the *Real Estate Weekly*.[47] According to Blakney (1992b), "The Director contended that the joint control of these publications coupled with Southam's existing control of two Vancouver dailies substantially lessened competition in the supply of newspaper advertising and real estate advertising services in various markets in the Vancouver area." The Tribunal found that Southam's acquisition of the *Courier* and *North Shore News* would not substantially lessen competition for advertising between Southam's-owned dailies and the community newspapers in the Vancouver area, but that the acquisition of the *North Shore News* and the *Real Estate Weekly* (which also served the North Shore) would substantially lessen competition for real estate advertising in that market. Counsel was directed by the Tribunal to submit further evidence and argument on an appropriate remedy to address the matter.

The *Hillsdown* and *Southam* Tribunal decisions were issued after the Director released the *Merger Enforcement Guidelines*. The Tribunal is clearly not bound by the *Guidelines*, and in the *Hillsdown* decision it seemed to take issue with both the Director's interpretation of the phrase "substantial lessening of competition" and the Director's interpretation of the efficiency-market power tradeoff analysis described in section 96. With respect to the former, in evaluating whether the merger would substantially lessen competition, the Tribunal rejected applying a rigid quantitative test (discussed in the *Guidelines*) to determine if the merged firm could raise price by five percent over two years.[48] With respect to section 96, it rejected the Director's position that proven efficiency gains from the merger should be balanced only against allocative inefficiencies or deadweight losses. Rather, the Tribunal indicated that it

---

[47] S*ee Canada (Director of Investigation and Research) v. Southam Inc.* (1992) 43 C.P.R. (3d) 161 (Comp. Trib.).

[48] See Blakney (1992a, p. 8). Interestingly, in the discussion of market definition in the *Laidlaw* decision, the Competition Tribunal indicated that it would not necessarily accept the Director's primary market definition criterion. "The Tribunal wishes to emphasize that the above discussion of the respondent's expert evidence should not be taken as an acceptance that the 5% price rise criterion is necessarily a useful one even in a merger case. While the test of a non-transitory significant price increase may be conceptually useful, what percentage will be significant and what period of time will satisfy the test of non-transitoriness can only be determined by reference to the facts of a particular case."

would not exclude wealth or distribution effects from its assessment of the impact of a merger in the context of a section 96 welfare tradeoff analysis.

In 1998, the Director made an application to the Competition Tribunal contesting the attempt by Superior Propane to acquire ICG Propane. These two companies were the principal Canadian suppliers of propane and propane related equipment. In the application, the Director argued that ICG Propane and Superior Propane competed in a large number of local geographic markets. It was alleged in the complaint that in a number of these local markets, the transaction would result in a monopoly, and that in many other markets the market shares of the combined firm would be greater than 65 percent. The Director argued that "the Merger would likely lessen or prevent competition substantially in the supply of propane, equipment and service maintenance of propane equipment and accessories to consumers, due in part to the merged entity's extremely high post-merger market share . . . the high barriers to entry and the fact that remaining competitors cannot, in many markets, be relied upon to constrain or reduce prices given the above factors and the frequency of interdependent behaviour of the propane industry in Canada."[49]

The Tribunal concluded in its decision in 2000 (paragraph 314) that the merger "is likely to lessen competition substantially in many local markets and for national account customers and that the merger is likely to prevent competition substantially in Atlantic Canada."[50] However, the Tribunal went on to argue that the efficiencies that were likely to result from the merger would exceed the deadweight loss resulting from the reduction of competition. Adopting a total surplus standard, the Tribunal approved the merger. Thus, the Tribunal rejected the suggestion of the Bureau that it should consider the distributional effects of the merger in evaluating efficiencies, and in particular whether the merger would redistribute income away from those less wealthy.

The Commissioner appealed this decision to the Federal Court of Appeal. As discussed in Trebilcock et al. (2002, p. 150), the Federal Court of Appeal held that "the effects of a merger, for purposes of section 96, should not be confined to dead-weight losses but should properly take into account redistributive effects as between

---

[49] See paragraph 39 of the Fresh as Amended Notice of Application, Director of Investigation and Research v. Superior Propane Inc., available on the Competition Tribunal's website at www.ct-tc.gc.ca/english/cases/propane/propane.html.

[50] See *Canada (Director of Investigation and Research) v. Superior Propane* (2000) 7 C.P.R. (4th) 385.

consumers and the merging parties." The Federal Court of Appeal set aside the Tribunal's decision, and the case was remitted to the Competition Tribunal for redetermination. In its subsequent decision in 2002, the Tribunal again approved the merger, concluding in paragraph 371 that "under any reasonable weighting scheme, the gains in efficiency of $29.2 million are greater than and offset all of the effects of lessening and prevention of competition attributable to the merger under review."

Recently, in 2000, the Commissioner made an application to the Tribunal in response to the acquisition of a landfill site in Ontario by Canadian Waste Services Holdings Inc., Canadian Waste Services Inc., and Waste Management Inc. In the application, the Commissioner argued that this acquisition would likely result in a substantial lessening or prevention of competition in the disposal of non-hazardous waste in the Greater Toronto Area and the Chatham-Kent Area, and in the associated markets for waste collection. In its 2001 Reasons and Order, the Tribunal decided that the transaction would prevent competition substantially in both areas. The divestiture of the acquired landfill was subsequently ordered.[51]

X. VERTICAL RESTRAINTS

Sections of the *Competition Act* dealing with vertical restraints can be found in Part VI of the Act, which is concerned with criminal offences in relation to competition, and Part VIII, which is concerned with matters reviewable by Tribunal. Section 61(1) in Part VI prohibits resale price maintenance (RPM), or an "attempt to influence upward, or to discourage the reduction of, the price at which any other person engaged in business in Canada supplies or offers to supply or advertises a product within Canada." It also prohibits a firm from refusing to supply a product to another firm because of that firm's low pricing policy. Section 61(6) prohibits a firm from attempting to induce a supplier not to supply another firm because of that firm's low pricing policy. Persons convicted under section 61(1) or section 61(6) are liable to a fine in the discretion of the court or to imprisonment for a term not exceeding five years or to both.

Section 61(10) lists four defences for a refusal to supply on account of a low pricing

---

[51] See *Commissioner of Competition v. Canadian Waste Services Holdings Inc.* (2001) Comp. Trib. 3, 28 March 2001.

policy of a firm: (1) the firm was using the supplier's products as loss leaders, (2) the firm was using the supplier's products to attract customers into its store in the hope of selling them other products, (3) the firm was using the supplier's products in misleading advertising, and (4) the firm was not providing the level of service that purchasers of the product might reasonably expect.

Table 4.1 shows that a significant proportion of combines prosecutions were for RPM or refusal to supply. The Crown's conviction rate for these offences was also relatively high (e.g. from 1954 to 1983, the Crown won 83 of 108 cases, or 77 percent). Given the prominent view among economists that RPM will often be efficiency enhancing and that situations where it can be used to promote either a dealers' or manufacturers' cartel are likely to be rare (see Carlton and Perloff, 2004, Chs. 12 and 19), there have been arguably too many RPM prosecutions.[52] Many economists would prefer to see RPM included as one of the practices reviewable by Tribunal rather than as a criminal offence.

Paquet and VanDuzer (1999, p. 56), in their review of the Competition Bureau's enforcement of the anti-competitive pricing provisions of the *Competition Act*, found that over the five year period from April 1, 1994, to March 31, 1999, there were 461 complaints regarding RPM. There were, however, only three formal enforcement proceedings undertaken with respect to these complaints.

Turning to vertical restraints reviewable by Tribunal, the *Competition Act* contains sections dealing with refusal to deal (section 75), consignment selling (section 76), exclusive dealing, tied selling, and market restriction (section 77). There have been two refusal to deal cases that have come before the Competition Tribunal, *The Director of Investigation and Research v. Chrysler Canada Ltd.* and *The Director of Investigation and Research v. Xerox Canada Ltd.*[53] These cases are important since they provide some indication of how the Tribunal defines relevant markets and

---

[52] As noted by Trebilcock et al. (2002, p. 412), resale price maintenance has virtually per se status in Canada. "Unless one of the defences is engaged, the authorities need only show the existence of RPM to support a conviction; its explanation is unnecessary." This could help to explain the Crown's high conviction rate in RPM cases.

[53] See *Director of Investigation and Research v. Chrysler Canada Ltd.* (1989), 27 C.P.R. (3d) 1 (Comp. Trib.), and *Director of Investigation and Research v. Xerox Canada Inc.* (1990) 33 C.P.R. (3d) 83 (Comp. Trib.).

analyzes the competitive effects of vertical restraints.

Refusal to Deal: The Chrysler and Xerox Cases

The *Chrysler* case arose from the Director's application to the Tribunal pursuant to section 75 requesting an order against Chrysler Canada Ltd. requiring that it accept Richard Brunet as a customer on trade terms usual and customary to its relationship with Brunet for the supply of Chrysler parts.[54] Brunet operated a business in Montreal that exported automotive parts to markets outside of North America.

Brunet had its first dealings with Chrysler Canada in 1977, and it was uncontested that Brunet was encouraged by Chrysler Canada throughout his association with it to expand the sale of Chrysler Canada auto parts in the export market. However, Brunet was notified on October 8, 1986 that Chrysler Canada would no longer fill orders for Brunet, and that the U.S. Chrysler Export Sales Office would handle future requirements.

---

[54] Section 75 reads as follows:

> 75.(1) Where, on application by the Commissioner or a person granted leave under section 103.1, the Tribunal finds that
> (a) a person is substantially affected in his business or is precluded from carrying on business due to his inability to obtain adequate supplies of a product anywhere in a market on usual trade terms,
> (b) the person referred to in paragraph (a) is unable to obtain adequate supplies of the product because of insufficient competition among suppliers of the product in the market,
> (c) the person referred to in paragraph (a) is willing and able to meet the usual trade terms of the supplier or suppliers of the product, and
> (d) the product is in ample supply, and
> (e) the refusal to deal is having or is likely to have an adverse effect on competition in a market,
> the Tribunal may order that one or more suppliers of the product in the market accept the person as a customer within a specified time on usual trade terms unless, within the specified time, in the case of an article, any customs duties on the article are removed, reduced or remitted and the effect of the removal, reduction or remission is to place the person on an equal footing with other persons who are able to obtain adequate supplies of the article in Canada.

The element labelled (e) was not in the *Competition Act* at the time that the Director filed applications in the *Chrysler* and *Xerox* cases.

Because Brunet then attempted to source Chrysler parts through Montreal-area Chrysler dealers, Chrysler Canada instructed its dealers not to sell parts for export out of Canada.

The Tribunal was mainly concerned with whether elements (1)(a) and (1)(b) of section 75 were met in this case, and began this determination by considering the market definition. The Tribunal decided that "the starting point for the definition of 'product' under section 75 is the buyer's customers" and that the relevant product market would then be Chrysler auto parts.

Professor Ralph A. Winter, Chrysler's economic expert, submitted the position that

> the Tribunal should approach the definition of product and market not from the point of view of Brunet as a buyer, but from the viewpoint of determining whether Chrysler has substantial market power. This, he submits, can only be done by considering what Chrysler sells and with whom it competes. He concludes that the relevant market is synonymous with the worldwide sale of automobiles since the price of auto parts is established in conjunction with the pricing of vehicles. It is Winter's view that Chrysler's pricing of parts is constrained by the effect this can have on the sale of its vehicles and that it faces very stiff competition in the sale of its vehicles. Winter concludes that since Chrysler does not have substantial market power as a seller of vehicles, its decision to discontinue supplying Brunet was motivated by concerns for efficiency and not to increase its market power.[55]

The Tribunal rejected Winter's submission, stating that it was satisfied that a broad consideration of Chrysler's market power is not required in determining whether the specific elements of section 75 of the Act have been satisfied, but may be relevant in the Tribunal's exercise of its discretion. (Again, sub-section (e) was not an element of section 75 at the time of the Chrysler case.)

With respect to the market in which Brunet was a buyer, the Tribunal rejected Chrysler's submission that the market consists of both the U.S. and Canada, and that

---

[55] See the *Director of Investigation and Research v. Chrysler Canada Ltd.* (1989), *supra* at note 53.

Chrysler U.S. is the supplier and the exporters of Chrysler auto parts are the buyers. It found instead that the relevant market is Canada because market conditions in the U.S. and Canada are different and the differences are reflected in different parts prices.

Having determined that the relevant market was Chrysler auto parts available in Canada, the Tribunal turned to a consideration of whether Brunet was substantially affected in his business by the refusal of Chrysler Canada to supply Brunet with Chrysler auto parts. The Tribunal concluded that Brunet had lost sales and gross profits as a result of Chrysler Canada's actions, and thus that his business had been substantially affected. The Tribunal also concluded that Brunet was unable to obtain supplies because of inadequate competition in the market. The Tribunal therefore decided to grant the Director's application and it ordered Chrysler Canada to supply Brunet Chrysler parts under the usual trade terms as it had done up to October 1986.[56]

In reaching its conclusion, the Tribunal found that "Section 75 is different than other sections in Part VIII of the Act. The test for whether the elements in the section are satisfied is not the effect on competition or efficiency. These considerations enter, where applicable, in the exercise of discretion." From an economic perspective, one would wish to evaluate a refusal to deal in terms of its effect on competition and efficiency. Indeed, the purpose of the *Competition Act* is "to maintain and encourage competition in Canada in order to promote the efficiency and adaptability of the Canadian economy...", so the Tribunal's interpretation of section 75 caused some discomfort among competition policy experts. It is perhaps for these reasons that the Act was amended to include sub-section (e), requiring that a refusal to deal have or likely have an adverse effect on competition in the market in order for it to contravene the Act.

The *Xerox Canada Inc.* case arose from the Director's application to the Tribunal pursuant to section 75 requesting an order to require Xerox Canada Inc. to accept Exdos Corporation as a customer for the supply of certain Xerox copier parts. In 1982, Terry Reid, an employee of Xerox, and Xerox agreed that it would be mutually advantageous if Reid left Xerox and created Exdos with the purpose of purchasing used Xerox machines, refurbishing them and selling them in the second-hand market. Exdos had the exclusive right to purchase certain used photocopier models from

---

[56] Chrysler Canada appealed the decision of the Tribunal to the Federal Court of Appeal, but the Court dismissed the appeal on September 19, 1991.

Xerox, and Exdos was supposed to purchase the models covered by the contract only from Xerox. Exdos was originally allowed to purchase parts from Xerox at a 50 percent discount off list, later reduced to a 25 percent discount, and eventually eliminated. Almost from its beginning Exdos began purchasing used Xerox machines from sources other than Xerox, and purchased parts for the repair of these machines from Xerox. At the same time that Exdos was expanding its activities in the marketing and servicing of second-hand Xerox machines, independent service organizations (ISOs) were doing the same. They competed with Xerox in the provision of service for Xerox machines. The revenue from servicing these machines can exceed the revenue obtained from the original sale of the machine.

The Tribunal accepted that Xerox was the largest supplier of copiers in Canada, with a 90 percent share of copier placements at the high-volume end of the market, almost 50 percent of copier placements in the medium volume range, and about one-third of low-volume copier placements. The Tribunal stated that the evidence did not warrant the conclusion that Xerox had little market power in the copier market.

In January 1987, Xerox U.S. issued a policy which entailed a refusal to supply ISOs in the U.S. with 10 Series and any new product parts for resale. According to the Tribunal, "The ISO policy for the United States was clearly designed to undercut the viability of the ISOs and to preserve, if not enhance, the revenue derived by Xerox Corp. from the service aspect of its business." This policy was adopted by Xerox Canada in June 1988, and led to the refusal to supply Exdos. On August 26, 1988, Exdos was advised that Xerox would no longer sell it used equipment after September 26, 1988, and parts for resale or service would be unavailable after October 26, 1988. Xerox also informed other Canadian ISOs that they would no longer be allowed to purchase parts from Xerox for resale or service.

In terms of satisfying the elements of section 75, the Tribunal found that there was no dispute that parts were in adequate supply, that Exdos was willing and able to meet the usual trade terms, that Exdos was unable to obtain adequate supplies of the parts, and that the inability to obtain parts has had and will have a substantial effect on Exdos' business. The main competition issue, then, was product market definition and whether Exdos' inability to obtain adequate supplies of the product arose because of insufficient competition among suppliers of the product in the market. The Tribunal did not accept the submission of Xerox's expert economist that the relevant product in this case was the provision of a package of services which leads to the creation of an imaged piece of paper. Nor did it accept his view that the product market which was relevant for section 75 purposes should be determined by reference to the market in which Xerox competed, the end user market. The Tribunal also rejected the view that Xerox's actions in curtailing supply were motivated by competition in the copier market and would in the long run result in the intensification of competition.[57]

The Tribunal concluded that the relevant geographic market was Canada and that the relevant product market could be defined as parts for Xerox copiers. (The relevant submarket for purposes of the *Xerox* case was held to be parts for post-1983 model copiers.) It concluded that there was insufficient competition among suppliers of the product in the market that affected Exdos' ability to obtain supplies of the product, and therefore issued an order requiring Xerox to accept Exdos as a customer for post-1983 Xerox copier parts.

The Competition Tribunal took a similar approach in *Chrysler* and *Xerox*, including its way of defining the relevant market. It chose a rather narrow market definition that arguably will increase the chances of finding that a firm cannot obtain adequate supplies of a product because of "insufficient competition" and may increase the chances of finding that a business has been substantially affected by the refusal to deal. The Tribunal at the time did not have to find that there was a substantial lessening of competition under section 75.

Exclusive Dealing and Tied Selling

Under section 77 of the *Competition Act*, exclusive dealing means "(a) any practice whereby a supplier of a product, as a condition of supplying the product to a customer, requires that customer to (i) deal only or primarily in products supplied by or designated by the supplier or the supplier's nominee, or (ii) refrain from dealing in a specified class or kind of product except as supplied by the supplier or the nominee."[58]

---

[57] Xerox's expert economist also was of the view that an order under section 75 would cause a welfare loss to consumers by substituting inefficient distribution systems for efficient systems. See *Director of Investigation and Research v. Xerox Canada Inc.* (1990), *supra* at note 53.

[58] Under sub-section 77(1)(b), exclusive dealing also includes "any practice whereby a supplier of a product induces a customer to meet a condition set out in subparagraph (a)(i) or (ii) by offering to supply the product to the customer on more favourable terms or conditions if the customer agrees to meet the condition set out in either of those subparagraphs."

Also under section 77, tied selling means "(a) any practice whereby a supplier of a product, as a condition of supplying the product (the "tying" product) to a customer, requires that customer to (i) acquire any other product from the supplier or the supplier's nominee, or (ii) refrain from using or distributing, in conjunction with the tying product, another product that is not of a brand or manufacture designated by the supplier or the nominee."[59]

In order for the Tribunal to make an order under section 77, the requirements are somewhat different than they are for section 75. In the cases of exclusive dealing and tied selling,

> Where, on application by the Commissioner or a person granted leave under section 103.1, the Tribunal finds that exclusive dealing or tied selling, because it is engaged in by a major supplier of a product in a market or because it is widespread in a market, is likely to
> (a) impede entry into or expansion of a firm in the market,
> (b) impede introduction of a product into or expansion of sales of a product in the market, or
> (c) have any other exclusionary effect in the market,
> with the result that competition is or is likely to be lessened substantially, the Tribunal may make an order directed to all or any of the suppliers against whom an order is sought prohibiting them from continuing to engage in that exclusive dealing or tied selling and containing any other requirement that, in its opinion, is necessary to overcome the effects thereof in the market or to restore or stimulate competition in the market.

The ability of a person granted leave under section 103.1 to make an application to the Tribunal under sections 75 and 77 of the *Competition Act* has only been in place with the coming into force of Bill C-23 on June 21, 2002.

There have been few cases involving allegations of exclusive dealing or tied selling

---

[59] Tied selling also means "(b) any practice whereby a supplier of a product induces a customer to meet a condition set out in subparagraph (a)(i) or (ii) by offering to supply the tying product to the customer on more favourable terms or conditions if the customer agrees to meet the condition set out in either of those subparagraphs."

heard by the Tribunal. In the *Director of Investigation and Research v. The NutraSweet Company* (1990), the Tribunal accepted the Director's application for an order under section 77. The Tribunal concluded that NutraSweet "has induced exclusive dealing with its aspartame customers through its financial incentives or fidelity rebates, and its exclusivity clauses. These inducements amount to a practice. NSC is a major supplier and this exclusive dealing has lessened, and is likely to lessen, competition substantially." The Tribunal rejected the Director's submission that NutraSweet had engaged in tied selling because "as a condition of supplying the trademark (the NutraSweet brand name and logo) to a customer, the respondent requires that the customer purchase another of its products, namely aspartame, and refrain from using the aspartame of any other producer in conjunction with the trademark."[60] (The *NutraSweet* case is discussed in more detail in Section V of this chapter.)[61]

In the *Tele-Direct* case, the Director alleged that Tele-Direct had engaged in the anti-competitive practice of tied selling.[62] Tele-Direct created and supplied the Yellow Pages telephone advertising directory which telephone companies in Canada were required to supply to their subscribers along with a white pages directory. It charged advertising customers a single price for placing advertisements in the Yellow Pages directory. In response to consultants who developed a business of advising major advertisers with respect to their advertising requirements, generally with the consultant being paid out of savings from a reduction in Yellow Pages advertising, Tele-Direct adopted a policy of refusing to accept instructions from consultants on behalf of a client. The Director contended that the supply of advertising services (by the consultants) was a product separate from the supply of advertising space. Tele-Direct was requiring advertising customers to refrain from using the advertising services of consultants as a condition of supplying advertising space in the Yellow Pages directory and consequently engaged in tied selling, which substantially lessened competition. The Competition Tribunal agreed, citing the majority decision of the U.S. Supreme

---

[60] See pages 99–100 of *Director of Investigation and Research v. The NutraSweet Co.* (1990), *supra* at note 24.

[61] In a more recent case that is still ongoing, *Commissioner of Competition v. Canada Pipe Co. Ltd.*, violations of the abuse of dominance and exclusive dealing provisions of the Act have been alleged.

[62] See *Director of Investigation and Research v. Tele-Direct (Publications) Inc.* (1977), *supra* at note 33.

Court in *Jefferson Parish v. Hyde* as the appropriate definition of whether one or two products are involved.[63]

Market Restriction

Under section 77, market restriction means "any practice whereby a supplier of a product, as a condition of supplying the product to a customer, requires that customer to supply any product only in a defined market, or exacts a penalty of any kind from the customer if he supplies any product outside a defined market." In the case of market restriction, the Tribunal may make an order prohibiting market restriction if it is found that it is engaged in by a major supplier or it is widespread in relation to a product, and is likely to substantially lessen competition in relation to the product. Market restriction clearly encompasses geographic territorial restraints (e.g., exclusive territories). It is unclear whether market restriction might also apply to a product market. There have yet to be any Competition Tribunal cases involving market restriction.

Other Vertical Restraint Cases

Between 1975, the year in which tied selling, exclusive dealing and market restriction were made civilly reviewable on a rule of reason basis by the Restrictive Trade Practices Commission (RTPC), and 1986, there was only one case involving exclusive dealing, *Director of Investigation and Research v. Bombardier Ltd. (1980)*, and one case involving tied selling, *Director of Investigation and Research v. BBM Bureau of Measurement* (1981).[64] In the former case, the RTPC found that Bombardier's practice of exclusive dealing in the distribution of its snowmobile products did not substantially lessen competition in the markets for snowmobile products. "The evidence establishes that there has been easy entry into the market. There has been an expansion of sales and dealerships by Bombardier's competitors. There is no evidence

---

[63] See *Jefferson Parish Hospital No. 2 v. Hyde* 466 U.S. 2, 104 S Ct 1551, 80 L Ed 2d 2 (1984). The test of whether there are two products involved considers whether there are separate demands for the two products, and not on the functional relationship between the two products. See Section VIII.D of the Competition Tribunal's decision in *Tele-Direct*.

[64] *Director of Investigation and Research v. Bombardier Ltd.* (1980), 53 C.P.R. (2d) 47; *Director of Investigation and Research* v. *BBM Bureau of Measurement* (1981), 60 C.P.R. (2d) 26 (Rest. Trade Pract. Comm.—Combines).

that competition at the manufacturing level was substantially affected by Bombardier's exclusive dealings in the markets covered by the application."[65] In the latter case, the RTPC found that the purchase of BBM's radio audience data was tied to the purchase of its television audience data, and that its tying arrangement lessened competition in the market.

Consignment Selling

Section 76 deals with consignment selling and permits the Tribunal to prohibit it where it finds that consignment selling has been introduced by a supplier for the purpose of (a) controlling the price at which a dealer in the product supplies the product, or (b) discriminating between consignees or between dealers to whom he sells the product for resale and consignees.

Consignment selling was one of the issues addressed by the RTPC in its broad investigation of competition in the Canadian petroleum industry, although it was not being considered as part of a section 31 (now section 76) case. Under one type of consignment program used by Gulf and Imperial Oil, the dealer was provided with a fixed commission. Gulf and Imperial Oil set the retail price by instructing dealers to post a certain price. Thus, changes in the retail price affected the profit margins of Gulf and Imperial, and not the dealer's commission. Shell used this approach until 1980, and then adopted a program where it set a maximum price, with the dealer free to set lower prices which would reduce the dealer's commission. The Director argued that the refiner's principal motive for using consignment selling was to achieve resale price maintenance, while the refiners argued that consignment selling was used to allow them to lower their wholesale prices as required by market conditions. According to the RTPC (1986, p. 364) the Director recommended that "Suppliers of motor fuels and affiliates be prohibited from obtaining direct or indirect control over retail prices of motor fuels at any marketing outlets other than outlets that the supplier owns and operates directly."

The RTPC concluded that "Some consignment programs do give the supplying refiner control over retail prices and are objectionable on that score. Any doubt or ambiguity about the dealers' authority over their prices is also a cause for concern, particularly in

---

[65] *Director of Investigation and Research v. Bombardier Ltd.* (1980), *id.* at 48.

the light of other characteristics of support programs."[66] And in the "Conclusions and Recommendations" chapter of its report (p. 465), the RTPC stated that "The Commission is concerned about the trend over the last decade towards greater centralization in the hands of refiners of the power to set pump prices. Supply arrangements under which refiners obtain partial or complete control over the retail prices of customers with whom they would otherwise compete at the retail level tend to lessen competition." It seems that had the Director sought an order prohibiting consignment selling under section 31, the RTPC may have been prepared to grant it.

XI. DECEPTIVE MARKETING PRACTICES

Sections 52 to 55 of the *Competition Act* cover a range of possibly deceptive marketing practices. These include false or misleading representations, deceptive telemarketing, deceptive notice of winning a prize, double ticketing, operating a "multi-level marketing plan," and pyramid selling.[67] Fines or imprisonment are the penalties prescribed for violation of these sections of the *Competition Act*.

On March 18, 1999, Bill C-20's amendments to the *Competition Act* came into effect. This bill, in part, created a civil process to "enable the Bureau to seek court orders to stop misleading advertising and deceptive marketing practices, while retaining criminal law for the most serious cases of deliberate misrepresentation."[68] Deceptive marketing practices covered by section 74 of the Act include misrepresentations to the public, bait and switch, sales above advertised price, and certain practices in relation to promotional contests.

---

[66] See RTPC (1986, pp. 357–370).

[67] See Addy (1991) for a review of deceptive marketing practices and discussion of relevant cases.

[68] See Commissioner of Competition, *Annual Report of the Commissioner of Competition for the Year Ending March 31, 1999*, p. 29.

Chapter 4

XII. SUMMARY

Canadian competition law has undergone numerous changes since the first *Act for the Prevention and Suppression of Combinations Found in Restraint of Trade* was passed in 1889. During much of its history, enforcement of competition law in Canada, particularly the merger provisions, has been difficult. The changes to competition law incorporated in the *Competition Act*, and importantly the creation of Part VIII, Matters Reviewable by Tribunal, should have improved the Commissioner's ability to challenge anti-competitive mergers and anti-competitive behaviour.

As part of the Commissioner's enforcement effort, guidelines have been issued which set out in some detail the Commissioner's enforcement policy with respect to price discrimination, predatory pricing, abuse of dominance, intellectual property, and merger. The latter document also contains a discussion of market definition criteria that the Commissioner will use in competition cases.

Between 1986, the year in which the Competition Tribunal was created, and 2001, relatively few cases were actually brought to the Tribunal by the Director/Commissioner. Between 1986 and 2001, there were only four Tribunal decisions that involved contested applications in abuse of dominance cases. (Two other abuse cases were settled by Tribunal consent orders.) There have also been two refusal to deal cases heard by the Tribunal, and a handful of Tribunal cases involving allegations of exclusive dealing and tied selling. Between 1986 and 1991, only nine applications involving merger cases were made to the Tribunal. Between 1992 and 2002, there were 30 applications to the Tribunal regarding merger cases, involving both consent orders and contested applications. In large part, the Commissioner's concerns regarding a possible lessening of competition caused by a proposed merger are usually addressed in negotiations between the Commissioner and the parties to the merger.

Certain aspects of competition policy, such as the conspiracy and misleading advertising provisions of the *Competition Act*, have been rigorously enforced in the past and will likely continue to be rigorously enforced in the future. Other aspects of competition policy enforcement, such as the anti-competitive pricing provisions of the *Competition Act*, have given rise to concerns among some members of the business community and Parliament in the past. These provisions may be the subject of both amendment and enhanced Competition Bureau enforcement efforts in the future.

REFERENCES

Addy, George N. 1991. "Deceptive Marketing Practices," in R.S. Khemani and W.T. Stanbury, eds., *Canadian Competition Policy at the Centenary*. Halifax: Institute for Research on Public Policy.

Areeda, Philip and Donald Turner. 1975. "Predatory Pricing and Related Practices under Section 2 of the Sherman Act," *Harvard Law Review* 88: 697–733.

Blakney, John F. 1992a. "Ontario Meat Rendering Merger: Competition Tribunal Turns Down Dir Divestiture Application," *Canadian Competition Policy Record* 13:6–10.

Blakney, John F. 1992b. "Competition Tribunal Decides Southam B.C. Newspapers Merger Case," *Canadian Competition Policy Record* 13:1–2.

Carlton, Dennis W. and Jeffrey M. Perloff. 2004. *Modern Industrial Organization*, Fourth Edition. New York: Pearson Education.

Chandler, Harry and Robert Jackson. 2000. "Beyond Merriment and Diversion: The Treatment of Conspiracies under Canada's Competition Act," Available on the Competition Bureau website at http://competition.ic.gc.ca/epic/internet/incb–bc.nsf/en/ct01767e.html.

Crampton, Paul S. 1991. "Relevant Market Analysis in Recent Merger Branch Decisions," in R.S. Khemani and W.T. Stanbury, eds., *Canadian Competition Policy at the Centenary*. Halifax: Institute for Research on Public Policy.

Commissioner of Competition. 1999–2003. *Annual Report of the Commissioner of Competition*. Ottawa: Competition Bureau.

Competition Bureau. 2000. *Intellectual Property Enforcement Guidelines*. Ottawa: Competition Bureau.

Competition Bureau. 2001a. *Enforcement Guidelines on the Abuse of Dominance Provisions (Sections 78 and 79 of the Competition Act)*. Ottawa: Competition Bureau.

Competition Bureau. 2001b. *Draft Enforcement Guidelines: The Abuse of Dominance Provisions (Sections 78 and 79 of the Competition Act) as Applied to the Retail Grocery Industry*, Ottawa: Competition Bureau.

Competition Bureau. 2001c. *Draft Enforcement Guidelines on: The Abuse of Dominance in the Airline Industry*, Ottawa: Competition Bureau.

Competition Bureau. 2002. "Draft Enforcement Guidelines for Illegal Trade Practices: Unreasonably Low Pricing Policies."

Competition Bureau. 2003. *The Merger Enforcement Guidelines as Applied to a Bank Merger*. Ottawa: Competition Bureau.

Director of Investigation and Research. 1981. *The State of Competition in the Canadian Petroleum Industry*. Ottawa: Minister of Supply and Services Canada.

Director of Investigation and Research. 1984–1991. *Annual Report of the Director of Investigation and Research*. Ottawa: Government of Canada.

Director of Investigation and Research. 1991. *Merger Enforcement Guidelines*. Ottawa: Minister of Supply and Services Canada. Reproduced with the permission of the Minister of Public Works and Government Services, 2004.

Director of Investigation and Research. 1992a. *Predatory Pricing Enforcement Guidelines*. Ottawa: Minister of Supply and Services Canada. Reproduced with the permission of the Minister of Public Works and Government Services, 2004.

Director of Investigation and Research. 1992b. *Price Discrimination Enforcement Guidelines*. Ottawa: Minister of Supply and Services Canada. Reproduced with the permission of the Minister of Public Works and Government Services, 2004.

Director of Investigation and Research. 1995. *Strategic Alliances under the Competition Act*. Ottawa: Minister of Supply and Services Canada.

Draper, Gary and Douglas West. 1999–2000. "Evaluating Challenges to Non–price Vertical Restraints," *Canadian Competition Record* 19: 86–97.

Dunlop, Bruce, David McQueen, and Michael Trebilcock. 1987. *Canadian Competition Policy: A Legal and Economic Analysis*. Toronto: Canada Law Book Inc.

Eckert, Andrew and Douglas S. West. 2002. "Predation in the Airline Industry: The Canadian Antitrust Approach," *The Antitrust Bulletin* 47: 217–242.

Economic Council of Canada. 1969. *Interim Report on Competition Policy*. Ottawa: Queen's Printer.

Gorecki, Paul K. and W.T. Stanbury. 1979. "Canada's *Combines Investigation Act*: The Record of Public Law Enforcement, 1889–1976," in J. Robert S. Prichard, W.T. Stanbury, and Thomas A. Wilson, eds., *Canadian Competition Policy: Essays in Law and Economics*. Toronto: Butterworths.

Gorecki, Paul K. and W.T. Stanbury. 1984. *The Objectives of Canadian Competition Policy, 1888–1983*. Montreal: The Institute for Research on Public Policy.

Green, Christopher. 1990. *Canadian Industrial Organization and Policy*. Third Edition. Toronto: McGraw–Hill Ryerson Ltd.

Howard, John L. and William T. Stanbury. 1990. "Oligopoly Power, Co–ordination, and Conscious Parallelism," in Frank Mathewson, Michael Trebilcock, and Michael Walker, eds., *The Law and Economics of Competition Policy*. Vancouver: The Fraser Institute.

Joskow, Paul and Alvin Klevorick. 1979. "A Framework for Analyzing Predatory

Pricing Policy," *Yale Law Journal* 89: 213–270.

Krattenmaker, T. and S. Salop. 1986. "Anticompetitive Exclusion: Raising Rivals' Costs to Achieve Power over Price," *Yale Law Journal* 96: 209–295.

Maule, Christopher J. and Thomas W. Ross. 1989. "Canada's New Competition Policy," *George Washington Journal of International Law and Economics* 23: 59–109.

McFetridge, Donald. 1990. "Predatory and Discriminatory Pricing," in Frank Mathewson, Michael Trebilcock, and Michael Walker, eds., *The Law and Economics of Competition Policy*. Vancouver: The Fraser Institute.

Public Policy Forum. 2004. *National Consultation on the Competition Act Final Report*.

Restrictive Trade Practices Commission. 1986. *Competition in the Canadian Petroleum Industry*. Ottawa: Minister of Supply and Services Canada.

Rowley, J.W. and W.T. Stanbury, eds. 1978. *Competition Policy in Canada: Stage II, Bill C–13*. Montreal: Institute for Research on Public Policy.

Stanbury, William T. 1991. "Legislation to Control Agreements in Restraint of Trade in Canada: Review of the Historical Record and Proposals for Reform," in R.S. Khemani and W.T. Stanbury, eds., *Canadian Competition Law and Policy at the Centenary*. Halifax: Institute for Research on Public Policy. Reprinted with permission of the Institute for Research on Public Policy.

Stanbury, William T. 1992. "An Assessment of the Merger Review Process under the *Competition Act*," *Canadian Business Law Journal* 20: 422–463.

Stanbury, W. T. 1998. "Expanding Responsibilities and Declining Resources: The Strategic Responses of the Competition Bureau, 1986–1996," *Review of Industrial Organization* 13: 205–241.

Standing Committee on Industry, Science and Technology. 2002. *A Plan to Modernize Canada's Competition Regime*. Ottawa: Public Works and Government Services Canada.

Stigler, George J. and Robert A. Sherwin. 1985. "The Extent of the Market," *Journal of Law and Economics* 28: 555–585.

Trebilcock, Michael J. 1990. "The Evolution of Competition Policy: A Comparative Perspective," in Frank Mathewson, Michael Trebilcock, and Michael Walker, eds., *The Law and Economics of Competition Policy*. Vancouver: The Fraser Institute.

Trebilcock, Michael, Ralph Winter, Paul Collins, and Edward Iacobucci. 2002. *The Law and Economics of Canadian Competition Policy*. Toronto: University of Toronto Press.

VanDuzer, J. Anthony and Gilles Paquet. 1999. *Anticompetitive Pricing Practices and the Competition Act: Theory, Law and Practice*. Available on the Competition Bureau's website at www.competition.ic.gc.ca.

Von Hohenbalken, Balder and Douglas S. West. 1984. "Predation among Supermarkets: An Algorithmic Locational Analysis," *Journal of Urban Economics* 15: 244–257.

Von Hohenbalken, Balder and Douglas S. West. 1986. "Empirical Tests for Predatory Reputation," *Canadian Journal of Economics* 19: 160–178.

Williamson, Oliver E. 1968. "Economies as an Antitrust Defense: The Welfare Tradeoffs," *American Economic Review* 58: 18–34.

CHAPTER 5

REGULATION

I. INTRODUCTION

Most industries in Canada are subject to some form of direct or indirect regulation by government. This chapter will be concerned with "economic regulation," defined by the Economic Council of Canada (1981, p. xi) as "the imposition of constraints, backed by the authority of a government, that are intended to modify economic behaviour in the private sector significantly." Carlton and Perloff (2004, Ch. 20) have discussed the objectives of regulators and types of economic regulation (e.g., price regulation, rate-of-return regulation), so the theory of regulation will not be reviewed here. Rather, this chapter will examine some of the most studied cases of regulation in Canada: regulation of telecommunications and transportation industries.

In examining the regulation and deregulation of these industries, attention will be given to the history of regulation affecting these industries as well as to the economic analysis that promoted deregulation. The economic analysis of deregulation is important since there will be calls to reregulate telecommunications or transportation industries should they face persistent financial problems or if competition fails to restrain future price increases. One would like to know whether any future economic problems confronting these industries are due to deregulation or due to some necessary restructuring brought about by competitive forces. If the latter is the case, deregulation might actually enhance the ability of these industries to adjust.

The move to deregulate a number of industries in Canada can be partly attributed to similar moves that took place in the U.S. (e.g., the *Airline Deregulation Act* of 1978 and the breaking up of AT&T in 1982, with its implications for enhanced competition in the provision of long distance calling services). An opportunity to promote regulatory reform was also provided by the Economic Council of Canada's "Regulation Reference." In 1978, Prime Minister Trudeau formally requested that the Economic Council of Canada "undertake a number of studies of specific areas of government regulation which appear to be having a particularly substantial impact on the Canadian economy." The Economic Council's final report was produced in 1981, and specific recommendations were made regarding the regulation of trains, trucks, taxicabs, the airline industry, the telecommunications industry, agriculture, tidal fisheries, environmental pollution, occupational health and safety, and occupations. The Economic Council's report will be referred to throughout this chapter, as will the moves made by the U.S. to deregulate various industries.

In the next section, telecommunications regulation in Canada will be discussed. Section III contains a review of transportation regulation in Canada, with a particular focus on railway, airline and trucking regulation. Section IV briefly surveys other regulated industries in Canada, including agricultural and public utility industries, while Section V contains a summary and some concluding remarks.

II. TELECOMMUNICATIONS REGULATION IN CANADA

The Bell Telephone Company of Canada was incorporated by an act of Parliament in 1880, and it was chartered to provide telephone service throughout Canada. Other telephone companies serving the maritime provinces were formed in the 1880s; Bell withdrew from the maritimes, preferring to concentrate on Ontario and Quebec. In Alberta, Saskatchewan, and Manitoba, telephone operations were acquired by provincial governments in 1908 and 1909 and organized as Crown corporations. Telephone service in B.C. was provided by B.C. Telephone, a subsidiary of U.S.-based GTE.[1]

Telephone companies acted as regional monopolies in the provision of local and long distance telephone services. In order to interconnect the regional telephone companies to form a long distance network, the telephone companies created the Telephone Association of Canada in 1921, which was replaced by the Trans-Canada Telephone System (TCTS). The TCTS completed a trans-continental long-distance telephone network in 1931. The members of TCTS would make decisions regarding inter-provincial long-distance rates and the division of revenues generated by inter-provincial long distance. Inter-provincial long-distance rates were not subject to any regulation until the late 1970s, when the CRTC announced that it would examine TCTS rates (see Stanbury and Thompson, 1982, p. 55). In 1983, the TCTS was renamed Telecom Canada and it had nine major telephone companies and Telesat Canada as members.[2] Telesat Canada was created by the federal government in 1969 and its purpose was to provide domestic satellite service. Its first satellite was launched in 1973. Telesat's system

---

[1] This brief history was obtained from Strick (1990).
[2] Telesat Canada joined TCTS in 1977.

transmitted voice, data, facsimile, television, and radio signals and was interconnected to the land-based telephone system.[3] Telecom Canada was replaced by Stentor in 1992. The federal government sold a majority interest in Telesat Canada to a consortium controlled by the Stentor-member telephone companies in 1991.[4]

Teleglobe Canada was established as a Crown corporation in 1950, and its purpose was to provide facilities for overseas telecommunications. Teleglobe was privatized in 1987 with its purchase by Memotec Data Inc.

According to Globerman (1988, p. 5), there were approximately 120 terrestrial telephone carriers operating in Canada in 1982. However, Telecom Canada member companies accounted for 95 percent of total telephone carrier revenue.

CNCP Telecommunications was created as a partnership between the telecommunications branches of Canadian National and Canadian Pacific railways. Originally, CNCP provided telegraph services and operated a nationwide microwave system that offered private-line and data communication services for business. CNCP was not allowed to provide general long-distance services in competition with the established telephone companies. In 1990, CNCP Telecommunications was renamed Unitel Communications, with CP Ltd. owning 60 percent and Rogers Communications owning 40 percent (which it acquired in 1984).[5]

Regulation of the telecommunications industry began in 1906, when Bell Canada's rates were made subject to the approval of the Board of Railway Commissioners under the *Railway Act*. The authority to regulate telephone companies under federal jurisdiction was transferred to the Canadian Transport Commission in 1967, and then to the Canadian Radio-Television and Telecommunications Commission (CRTC) in 1976.[6]

---

[3] See Globerman (1988, pp. 4-6).

[4] See Stanbury (1996a, p. 146).

[5] In 1993, AT&T purchased a 20 percent share of Unitel, and Rogers Communications' share was reduced to 32 percent. Rogers sold out of Unitel in 1995. See http://www.ketupa.net/rogers2.htm for a brief history of Rogers Communications. According to Stanbury's (1996b, p. 408) chronology of developments in Canadian telecommunications, in early 1996 Unitel's shares were to be split between the Bank of Nova Scotia (28 percent), Toronto Dominion Bank (23 percent), Royal Bank (16 percent), and AT&T (33 percent). Canadian Pacific and Rogers Communications received nothing for their 48 percent and 28 percent stakes in Unitel, respectively.

[6] See Strick (1990, p. 151).

Those telephone companies that are provincial Crown corporations (e.g. SaskTel) are regulated by the provincial government or by provincial public utility boards.

Besides telecommunications, the CRTC also has responsibility for regulating radio, television, and cable. The CRTC was created by the *Broadcasting Act of 1968* and is the successor to the Board of Broadcast Governors (created by the *Broadcasting Act of 1958*).[7] The CRTC's mandate with respect to broadcasting regulation is now found in the *Broadcasting Act of 1991*, while its telecommunications regulatory powers derive from the *Telecommunications Act* (1993) and *Bell Canada Act* (1987).

The CRTC will be guided by the statement of Canadian telecommunications policy that appears in section 7 of the *Telecommunications Act*:

> It is hereby affirmed that telecommunications performs an essential role in the maintenance of Canada's identity and sovereignty and that the Canadian telecommunications policy has as its objectives
>
> (a) to facilitate the orderly development throughout Canada of a telecommunications system that serves to safeguard, enrich and strengthen the social and economic fabric of Canada and its regions;
>
> (b) to render reliable and affordable telecommunications services of high quality accessible to Canadians in both urban and rural areas in all regions of Canada;
>
> (c) to enhance the efficiency and competitiveness, at the national and international levels, of Canadian telecommunications;
>
> (d) to promote the ownership and control of Canadian carriers by Canadians;
>
> (e) to promote the use of Canadian transmission facilities for telecommunications within Canada and between Canada and points outside Canada;
>
> (f) to foster increased reliance on market forces for the provision of telecommunications services and to ensure that regulation, where required, is efficient and effective;
>
> (g) to stimulate research and development in Canada in the field of telecommunications and to encourage innovation in the provision of telecommunications services;

---

[7] From 1932 to 1958, the Canadian Broadcasting Corporation regulated itself as well as privately-owned broadcasters.

(h) to respond to the economic and social requirements of users of telecommunications services; and

(i) to contribute to the protection of the privacy of persons.

CRTC regulation of telephone companies, for a number of years, was based on an allowed rate of return and a determined rate base.[8] Rates for individual services were not necessarily set to cover their costs; indeed, rates for long-distance services were established historically at levels designed to subsidize the rates for local telephone service. The Economic Council of Canada (1981) noted that "cross-subsidization" of local service rates by revenues from long-distance service was an important issue that was tied to the question of whether the CRTC should permit increased competition in the provision of long-distance services. Research for the Council supported the view that Bell's local rates were being substantially subsidized.[9]

Since 1979, there has been a progressive relaxation of restrictions on competition in the telecommunications industry in Canada.[10] In 1979, the CRTC approved CNCP's application for permission to interconnect CNCP facilities with those of Bell Canada for purposes of data communication and private-line voice communication. In 1981, CNCP was permitted similar interconnection in the B.C. Telephone operating territory. In 1982, the CRTC set out terms and conditions governing the attachment of subscriber provided terminal equipment (e.g., telephone sets) to the networks of all federally regulated telecommunications carriers. In 1985, the CRTC approved an application by B.C. Rail to compete with B.C. Telephone in the provision of certain private line and data communication services. The CRTC also allowed the interconnection of private local systems and public non-voice local systems to facilities of the federally regulated common carriers. However, in August 1985, the CRTC rejected an application by CNCP

---

[8] See Strick (1990, pp. 154–162) for a more detailed description of telephone rate regulation. Price cap regulation came into effect for the local services of incumbent telephone companies on January 1, 1998. See Industry Canada (2003, p. 6–16).

[9] See Fuss and Waverman (1981). Stanbury and Thompson (1982) report that Bell estimated that in 1980 the costs of local exchange service exceeded revenues from the flat-rate monthly billing by $710 million. This was largely made up by long-distance toll revenues that exceeded the cost of providing that service by $725 million. "Bell calculates that each $1 of toll revenues costs only $0.43 to produce. On the other hand, local services cost $1.84 to produce each $1 of revenue."

[10] The following summary is due to Globerman (1988, p. 9).

to compete with Bell Canada and B.C. Telephone in the provision of long-distance telephone service.

According to Strick (1990, p. 168), CNCP had argued that competition would reduce long-distance rates by an amount ranging from 10-20 percent for about 10 million telephone users. (See also Stanbury (1986) for a discussion of CNCP's position.) Bell Canada and B.C. Telephone opposed the application, arguing that competition in the provision of long-distance service would reduce their long-distance revenues and therefore their ability to subsidize local service rates. Blakney (1992a) notes that "in its 1985 decision, the CRTC found that CNCP Telecommunications would not be viable over a ten-year time horizon if it was required to make the contribution charge calculated by the Commission to provide an adequate offset representing the telephone companies' foregone contribution. The CRTC concluded that this finding provided a sufficient reason to deny CNCP's application and also to decline to set general entry terms."

The issues raised in the debate over long-distance competition in Canada were similar to the issues raised in the debate over increased competition in the telephone industry in the U.S. Until 1982, the telephone industry in the U.S. was virtually monopolized by one firm, AT&T, although some inroads were made by new firms during the 1960s and 1970s. In 1982, an agreement was reached regarding an antitrust complaint filed in 1974 by the Justice Department against AT&T and its subsidiary Western Electric. The relief prescribed in the Modified Final Judgment included (1) a requirement that AT&T divest itself of local operating companies, (2) that these companies provide equal access to all interexchange carriers, and (3) permission for AT&T to retain Long Lines, Western Electric, and Bell Labs. Thus, firms like MCI and GTE Sprint were allowed to interconnect with local networks on a basis equal to that of AT&T and to offer long-distance service in direct competition with AT&T. [11]

Throughout the period when new firms applied to the FCC for permission to compete in the long-distance market with AT&T, AT&T opposed the applications by arguing that it was a natural monopoly, that it enjoyed scale economies and high rates of productivity growth, that new entrants would engage in cream skimming (i.e., serve the most profitable parts of the market while leaving the unprofitable parts to AT&T), and that it

---

[11] For a detailed discussion of the history of new competition in the long-distance market in the U.S., see Brock (1981).

would be unable to maintain low local service rates because reduced long-distance revenue would impede its ability to subsidize local service.

The sort of arguments made by AT&T in opposing long-distance competition continued to be discussed in Canada in the wake of the CRTC's 1985 decision to reject increased long-distance competition in Canada. Globerman (1988) acknowledged that there was a concern held by some that the telecommunications industry was a natural monopoly and that without regulation, established carriers would charge monopoly prices. However, he noted that the available evidence did not support this view and that economies of scale seemed important only in the local loop portion of the industry. Globerman also rejected the argument that established carriers would use profits earned in regulated sectors of the industry (like local service) to subsidize predation against rival firms in competitive sectors (like long distance). Such an argument rested on the unsupported assumption that common carriers earned more than the cost of capital in the regulated sector. Globerman went on to discuss a further concern articulated by opponents of deregulation that the subsidization of local rates by long-distance revenues would break down because new entry in the long distance end of the market would force the reduction of long-distance rates. Globerman suggested that one way of preventing excessive entry induced by profits on long-distance service was to allow local service and long-distance rates to adjust to reflect cost of service.

Finally, Globerman discussed some possible costs of failing to deregulate telecommunications. These costs included the bypass of established carrier facilities by large business consumers of telecommunications services. Of particular concern was cross-border bypass through the U.S. There were also potential social welfare losses due to underpricing local service and overpricing long-distance service. Using U.S. estimates as a guide, Globerman (1986) came up with a crude estimate of welfare losses from telephone cross subsidies in Canada of around $2 billion per year. This estimate, he suggested, was roughly consistent with the estimate made by Peat Marwick in 1984 that a 40 percent toll rate reduction would have provided a net gain in consumer surplus of over $0.6 billion per year in Canada in 1982.

The public debate over competition in the provision of long-distance service was once again brought before the CRTC because of new applications by Unitel Communications Inc. and BC Rail Telecommunications/Lightel Inc. (BCRL) to provide long-distance telephone services.[12] On July 5, 1991, the CRTC concluded 53 days of public hearings into Unitel's and BCRL's applications. On June 12, 1992, the CRTC released its decision on the provision of competitive long-distance services by way of competitor interconnection with local and toll-switching facilities of federally regulated telephone companies. The decision "approves an open entry regime for long distance telecommunication competition involving both telephone company switch and local loop interconnections, service resale and the establishment of general conditions of entry for all potential competitors (including Unitel and BCRL)."[13] Financial terms were also set out for contribution charges to be paid by competitors to subsidize the local rates of the established telephone companies, and the terms of equivalent access were established. The CRTC decided that any firm willing to pay contribution charges and to pay for interconnection and related services would be allowed to enter the long-distance market. The economic viability of the entrant would no longer be a central concern.

Blakney (1992a) reported that the CRTC found that long distance competition was in the public interest, and that it was essential for general economic development and the efficient development of the telecommunications sector of the economy. The CRTC rejected the telephone companies' argument that the long-distance sector was a natural monopoly, and found that the evidence on scale economies in the long-distance industry was inconclusive. The CRTC also accepted that industry performance, as measured by customer responsiveness and product and price innovation, would be superior in a competitive environment.

The CRTC also approved Unitel's proposal that the contribution charge be discounted by a declining percentage until 1997 to reflect the fact that the established telephone companies had a market advantage and that customers of new entrants would not have equal access to them compared to established firms over the start-up period. The CRTC apparently also indicated that it did not expect long-distance competition to result in higher local rates over the next few years. The CRTC expected long-distance rates to fall

---

[12] Blakney (1991, p. 17) reports that established telephone companies contended before the CRTC that the interexchange and local exchange portions of their business constituted a natural monopoly. "The telephone companies used two principal arguments to support this proposition. Firstly, they argued that incumbent carriers' marginal costs of interexchange switching and transmission capacity would always necessarily be lower than the marginal costs of such facilities investments made by a new start-up firm having no interexchange plant base of significance to build upon. Secondly, they maintained that there are great future efficiencies to be gained from vertically integrated local and long-distance network components."

[13] See Blakney (1992a, p. 52).

in the future and it increased the pricing flexibility of the established telephone companies, in part to assist in achieving this objective.[14]

The coming into force of the *Telecommunications Act* in 1993 paved the way for a number of initiatives undertaken by the CRTC to increase competition in the telecommunications industry.[15] These have been summarised by Industry Canada (2003, p. 6-1) as follows:

> Through the licensing of Personal Communication Service (PCS) spectrum in 1995 under the *Radiocommunication Act*, two more competitors were allowed into the mobile cellular telephone market. In 1997, the CRTC announced the regulatory framework for competition in local telephone services. In 1998, the CRTC liberalized the public pay telephone service market. Also in 1998, the CRTC opened the facilities-based international telecommunications market to competition and established a new regulatory framework for all international services, thus fulfilling part of Canada's commitment in the World Trade Organization (WTO) Agreement on Basic Telecommunications Services. In further fulfilment of the WTO agreement, Canada ended Telesat Canada's monopoly on satellite telecommunications carriage, effective March 1, 2000.

One of the powers granted to the CRTC by the *Telecommunications Act* is the power to refrain from regulating a telecommunications service (called "forbearance" in the Act). Where the CRTC finds that a service or class of services provided by a Canadian carrier

---

[14] The established telephone companies affected by the CRTC's decision appealed that decision to the Federal Court of Appeal. They argued that the CRTC should have required that new long-distance carriers pay the full cost of interconnection with the telephone network rather than just 30 percent of the cost. The telephone companies were also concerned that the discount on the contribution charge given to new carriers was designed to equalize competition, and they contended that the *Railway Act* did not contemplate the CRTC influencing market structure. The Federal Court of Appeal denied the Appeal in December 1992. See Blakney (1992b).

[15] According to Industry Canada (2003, p. 6-3), the *Telecommunications Act* "consolidated and updated laws governing Canadian telecommunications, some of which dated from 1908. The legislation brought amendments to the *Radiocommunication Act*, and to the special acts relating to Bell Canada, BC Tel, Teleglobe Canada and Telesat Canada. It repealed the *National Telecommunications Powers and Procedures Act* and the *Telegraphs Act*, and those sections of the *Railway Act* which formerly dealt with telecommunications."

will be subject to competition sufficient to protect the interests of users, the Commission is instructed to refrain from regulating the service. The CRTC has used this power on a number of occasions. For example, in a series of decisions between 1994 and 1999, the CRTC decided not to regulate wireless services, including wireless services provided by non-telephone companies, Bell, BC Tel, Island Tel, MTT, MTS, NB Tel, NewTel, and Quebec-Telephone.[16] In 1998, it chose not to regulate certain telecommunication services offered by broadcast carriers, and in 1999, it chose not to regulate retail internet services. (See Industry Canada, 2003, Tables D-1 and D-2.)

While the CRTC has chosen forbearance for a number of telecommunications services, a number of the incumbent telephone companies' services remain subject to regulation. Large incumbent telephone companies include Aliant Telecom Inc., Bell Canada, MTS Communications Inc., SaskTel, and TELUS Communications Inc. According to the CRTC (2003, p. 7), regulated services include residential basic local services, business single and multi-line local services, local options and features, payphone, digital network access, local channels and competitor services.

Like the banking and airline industries, there are foreign ownership restrictions in place with respect to certain telecommunications firms. The *Telecommunications Act* (section 16) requires that Canadians own 80 percent of the shares of Canadian carriers that own telecommunications transmission facilities. Canada removed foreign ownership restrictions with respect to global mobile satellite services and submarine cables. Telesat Canada's monopoly on domestic and trans-border telecommunications carriage ceased on March 1, 2000, while Teleglobe's monopoly was terminated on October 1, 1998.[17]

As noted above, local telephone service was opened to facilities-based competition in 1997. It continues to be subject to regulation, although rate of return regulation was replaced by price cap regulation on January 1, 1998. The CRTC (2003, p. 38) has reported that there has been limited entry into the local and access segments of the telecommunications market since the introduction of local competition. Incumbents' local market shares by province continue to be quite high, ranging from 93.3 percent in Ontario to 100.0 percent in Saskatchewan in 2002. The CRTC (2003, p. 10) defines incumbent telephone companies as those that provided telecommunications services on a

---

[16] In 2002, the combined revenue market share of TELUS, Bell Wireless Alliance, and Rogers in the wireless industry was over 90 percent. See CRTC (2003, p. 62).

[17] See Industry Canada (2003, p. 6-9).

monopoly basis prior to the introduction of competition. Competitors are defined as non-incumbent telephone companies, and include facilities-based competitive service providers, resellers, payphone service providers, cable service providers, and utility telcos.

With respect to long distance service, there have been greater competitive inroads since competition in the provision of long distance services was opened up in 1992. The CRTC (2003, p. 24) reports that competitors' share of long distance revenues was 27 percent in 2002. Incumbents had an 80 percent share of residential long distance revenues, and 62 percent of business long distance revenues in 2002. With the exception of Northwestel, beginning in 1998 the CRTC declined to engage in rate regulation of incumbent long distance services. The CRTC (2003, p. 26) notes that there has been a continual reduction in long distance rates since the inception of competition in the provision of long distance services.

The telecommunications industry in Canada has clearly become more competitive since 1992–1993, with the allowance of competition in the provision of long distance services and the passage of the *Telecommunications Act*. Since 1992-1993, Canada has seen tremendous growth in both internet and wireless services, both of which have rates that the CRTC has declined to regulate. There is competition in the provision of internet services, with incumbent telephone companies holding a 41 percent share of internet access revenues in 2002 and cable companies holding a 35 percent share. There is also competition in the mobile part of the telecommunications industry, with the mobile share of telecommunications revenues growing from 21 percent to 23 percent of industry revenues in 2002. It remains to be seen to what extent increased competition in telecommunications markets will increase CRTC forbearance in the future.

III. TRANSPORTATION REGULATION

Almost all forms of transport in Canada have been subject to some type of regulation. From the mid-1800s to the mid-1980s, the federal government's transportation policy and regulations were intended to promote the development of a national transportation network. Arguably, however, many government regulations of transportation no longer served this purpose by the time that the Economic Council of Canada issued its report on regulation in 1981. Partly for this reason, most transportation industries were deregulated to a significant degree in the 1980s.

The regulation of transportation industries began with rail regulation, which originated in the first *Railway Act* of 1851.[18] This act stated that no toll could be charged until the Governor in Council had approved it. Regulatory responsibilities moved to the Railway Committee of the Privy Council in 1888 and to the Board of Railway Commissioners in 1903.

In the 1800s, the federal government initiated construction and helped fund the first transcontinental railway, what was later to become Canadian Pacific Railway (CPR). In 1923, the competitors of the CPR were nationalized into Canadian National Railway (CNR) because they were in financial difficulty. To provide Canada with transcontinental air service, legislation was adopted in 1937 creating Trans-Canada Airlines (TCA) as a subsidiary of CNR. TCA obtained almost a monopoly on domestic and international air service, and the Board of Transport Commissioners (later the Air Transport Board) was expected to maintain this policy by using its authority over the granting of licenses.

In the Economic Council of Canada's (1981, p. 14) view, the regulation of rail, with its high rates, facilitated the growth of a lower-cost motor carrier industry. The increasing competition that trucking provided to the railway industry led the latter in the 1930s to call for regulation of the trucking industry. The trucking industry, feeling the effects of the Depression in the 1930s, also requested that it be regulated so as to ensure stability and orderly growth. The provinces of Quebec, Ontario, British Columbia, and Manitoba complied with these requests for regulation of trucking.

Over the years, the other transportation industries such as marine transportation and commodity pipelines, have also been subject to federal regulation, and certain other modes of transportation, such as taxicab and intercity bus, were subject to municipal or provincial regulation. In this section, attention will be confined to the regulation of rail, air, and truck transportation.

---

[18] The following brief history of transport regulation in Canada was obtained from the Economic Council of Canada (1981).

Railway Regulation

In 1961, the MacPherson Commission recommended that freight rates be freed from regulation, and that carriers be allowed broad limits within which rates on commodities not subject to statutory freight rates could be set. This recommendation was made in recognition of the increased competition that the railroads faced, and the federal government largely implemented the recommendation in its *National Transportation Act* (NTA) of 1967. Railroads were permitted to set nongrain freight rates without the prior approval of the Canadian Transport Commission (CTC), the only requirement being that rates be compensatory (i.e., above "variable cost" as defined by the CTC). Where a shipper could show that it was a captive shipper (a shipper that lacked an alternative common carrier to the rail common carrier), the CTC was to ensure that rates fell within a relatively high maximum bound (i.e., "variable cost" plus 150 percent). Bonsor (1984) reported that up through 1984, the CTC had not conducted any investigation into whether or not a specific rate was below variable cost, and no shipper had been granted captive shipper status.

The NTA did not allow railways to raise the grain rates, which were subject to the Crow's Nest Pass Agreement on grain shipments and subsidies under the *Maritime Freight Rate Assistance Act*.[19] Railways were also prohibited from abandoning more than 30,000 kilometres of railway lines on the Prairies. Palmer (1988, p. 42) has argued that the growing competition from other modes of transportation meant that railways were unable to use their new rate-setting abilities to generate sufficient net revenue in some markets to cross-subsidize grain shipping.

The Crow's Nest Pass rates were originally agreed to by the Dominion of Canada and the CPR in 1897, and later contained in the *Railway Act*. These rates allowed grain and certain grain products to be transported by rail from western Canada to export points at a fraction of actual transport costs. According to the Economic Council of Canada (1981, p. 16), in 1977 only 32 percent of the variable costs were covered by users, 18 percent were covered by federal branch-line subsidies, and the remaining 50 percent were left to be absorbed by the railways.

Norrie (1983) has discussed some of the efficiency and equity implications of the Crow

---

[19] See Economic Council of Canada (1981, p. 15).

Rates. With respect to the efficiency implications, first, railways lost money on carrying grain at the Crow Rates, but they could not abandon this traffic. As a consequence, they had no incentive to invest in new facilities and equipment linked to the grain trade or to maintain existing facilities and equipment. By the early 1970s, the grain handling and distribution system was in poor condition: the boxcar fleet had shrunk and branch lines had deteriorated. In response to this, the federal government made branch line subsidy payments and committed nearly $700 million to upgrading the basic branch line network. It, along with the Canadian Wheat Board and the prairie provincial governments, also purchased or leased thousands of hopper cars. There were also government-financed port improvements. Norrie viewed these arrangements as ad hoc, incomplete, and inefficient.

A second efficiency consideration arises from the fact that because rail transport of grain was subsidized, more grain would be moved by rail as opposed to by unsubsidized trucks than is socially optimal, and too many collection points would be maintained as a result. A third efficiency consideration stems from the fact that freight rates held below cost imply that grain prices at the farm gate were higher than they would be in the absence of the Crow Rates (since a smaller deduction from the world price of grain needed to be made to cover transport costs). This can lead farmers to maintain land in production that would otherwise be uneconomic and it can also lead to less processing activity than would otherwise occur.

On February 8, 1982, the federal government announced its intention to rectify the problems created by the Crow Rates. It commissioned J.C. Gilson to find a means of implementing a new grain freight rate structure, and the federal government's initial transportation proposals of February 1, 1983 were based on Gilson's June 1982 report. These proposals came under attack and were significantly modified in the *Western Grain Transportation Act* (WGTA), passed in November 1983. According to Loyns, Carter and Peters (1991), the "Crow Benefit" payable to the railways was established as $695 million in 1981–82 dollars, and was applicable to the 1981–82 volume of movements of 31.5 million-tonnes. There were also increased transportation charges paid by farmers for grain shipments, but these payments were still below the variable cost of moving grain because of the federal subsidy. Since railways were paid the estimated cost of moving grain, Loyns et al. believed that they should have an incentive to provide rolling stock.

The National Transportation Agency (NTA), in its annual report for 1992, stated that its annual rate scales set the total rail transportation charges for the movement of grain from individual prairie shipping points to Canadian export ports. For each point, the total rate was divided to establish the rate the railways charged producers and the rate to be paid through federal government subsidies. In 1992, subsidy payments of $783.8 million under the WGTA were paid to CN, CP, BC Rail, Central Western Railway and the Southern Rails Cooperative. The WGTA also required the NTA to conduct reviews every four years to determine the cost of transporting western grain by rail. Furthermore, the WGTA required the NTA to monitor and audit railway maintenance expenditures on grain dependent branch lines and grain-related investment in railway equipment and plant to help "ensure an adequate, reliable and efficient railway transportation system that will meet future requirements for the movement of grain" (National Transportation Agency, 1992, p. 18).

Norrie (1983, p. 442) was critical of the WGTA in that it had the grain transportation subsidy paid to the railways instead of the shippers. In his view, "There is, in other words, to be no major, one-time corrective adjustment of statutory grain freight rates nor, consequently, of associated economic distributions. This feature of the Act, taken by itself, will perpetuate existing anomalies in crop mix, acreage decisions and industrial locations." It seems, then, that while the grain transportation problem had been partially addressed, the solution adopted by the government may not have been the most efficient one from an economic perspective.

The next major event in the history of railway regulation in Canada occurred in July 1985 with the release of *Freedom to Move*, a paper containing the Minister of Transport's recommendations for reform of transportation regulation. With respect to railway freight, the Minister recommended that (1) railways be required to publish their tariffs and to make them available for public scrutiny, and that (2) section 279 of the *Railway Act* that enabled the exchange of information among railways and the establishment of common rates among the railways, and section 32(2) of the *Transport Act* which dealt with agreed charges be repealed, and that confidential contracts between railways and shippers be permitted. These and other changes to railway regulation were incorporated in the *National Transportation Act, 1987*. According to Palmer (1991), until this Act was passed in 1987, "the railways had engaged in what was euphemistically referred to as collective rate-making. Despite the creative choice of phrase, most people recognized it for what it was: government-sanctioned collusion. And despite opposition from railway interests, Bill C-118 [the *National Transportation Act*] did away with collective ratemaking."

The *National Transportation Act* affected the regulation of transport by railway, by air, by water, by commodity pipeline, and by extra-provincial bus and truck. The Act declared that the objectives of a safe, economic, efficient and adequate network of viable and effective transportation services making the best use of all available modes of transportation at the lowest total cost are most likely to be achieved "when all carriers are able to compete, both within and among the various modes of transportation, under conditions ensuring that, having due regard to national policy and to legal and constitutional requirements...

(b) competition and market forces are, wherever possible, the prime agents in providing viable and effective transportation services,

(c) economic regulation of carriers and modes of transportation occurs only in respect of those services and regions where regulation is necessary to serve the transportation needs of shippers and travellers and such regulation will not unfairly limit the ability of any carrier or mode of transportation to compete freely with any other carrier or mode of transportation..."

In 1995, the regulation of grain transportation was brought under the *National Transportation Act* through Bill C-76. In the process, the Crow Benefit (the fraction of the freight rate paid by the government) was eliminated, the adjustment process for grain rates was revised, and statutory rates were changed to a rate cap.

In 1996, the *National Transportation Act 1987* was repealed and the *Canada Transportation Act* (CTA) was enacted.[20] The CTA reaffirmed the importance of competition among carriers, and maintained the reforms instituted in the *National Transportation Act 1987*. In addition, the CTA introduced several revisions which, according to Monteiro (2001, p. 3), (1) facilitated the entry of low cost carriers as feeders of traffic for the mainline carriers, (2) made rail rationalization less adversarial and facilitated sales to new operators, and (3) required federal railways to issue three-year network plans.

Railway transportation is covered in Part III of the CTA. Division II of Part III covers the construction and operation of railways, specifying the requirements for a Certificate of Fitness to construct or operate a railway, the general powers of railway companies, the

---

[20] A survey of recent changes to regulation in the rail, trucking, and air transport industries is given in Monteiro (2001).

rules for land transfers, and the approval requirements for the construction of railway lines and crossings. Division III discusses financial transactions, including mortgages issued by railway companies, documents dealing with rolling stock, and insolvent railway companies. Division IV concerns rates, tariffs and services, and Division V discusses transferring and discontinuing operations of railway lines. Division VI covers the transportation of grain.

The regulation of railway transportation under the CTA was the subject of two reviews in the late 1990s. In 1998, Justice Willard Z. Estey conducted a review of grain handling and transportation regulation. One of his recommendations was that a revenue cap replace the rate cap on grain freight rates. In 1999, a report by Arthur Kroeger on the implementation of the Estey review recommended a revenue cap that would initially reduce revenues by 12 percent from 1998 values. Other recommendations related to other aspects of the Estey review. Subsequently, the CTA was amended in 2000 to accommodate the recommendations of the Estey review and the Kroeger report. The amendments included a revenue cap, changes to the rationalization process regarding branch lines, and changes to the final offer arbitration process.

Trucking Regulation and Deregulation

In 1952, a Supreme Court of Canada decision gave the federal government the right to regulate all interprovincial and international trucking operations. As a result of this decision, Parliament passed the *Motor Vehicles Transport Act* of 1954, which gave the provinces the right to regulate all trucking, including interprovincial and intraprovincial trucking, provided that the same regulatory standards were applied to all trucking.[21]

According to the Economic Council of Canada (1981), all provinces controlled entry into interprovincial trucking, and all except Alberta controlled entry into intraprovincial for-hire trucking. Exemptions from licensing requirements were generally extended to private trucking, intraurban trucking, and the initial for-hire movement of farm, forest, and sea products. Licensing restrictions could cover the choice of freight that could be carried, routes that may be followed, origin and destination points for shipments, intermediate points that may be served, persons to be served, type of truck to be used, or frequency of service required. Any changes required approval of a provincial regulatory board.

---

[21] See Palmer (1991) and Bonsor (1984, pp. 84–86).

To gain entry into the for-hire trucking industry, a carrier had to show the regulatory board that its entry satisfied the test of "public convenience and necessity." This requirement has turned out to be a major obstacle to entry into the for-hire trucking industry, and it substantially raised the cost of entry.

All provinces, except Alberta, imposed some control on intraprovincial trucking rates. The provinces of Nova Scotia, New Brunswick, Ontario and Prince Edward Island only required that rates be filed with the regulatory board, while Newfoundland, Quebec and British Columbia required that rates be filed and approved. Saskatchewan prescribed a maximum rate for general merchandise, but excluded a number of commodities from rate control, while Manitoba prescribed intraprovincial rates, with approved exceptions. Only Newfoundland and Quebec required approval for interprovincial rates.

The Economic Council of Canada (1981) summarized the effects of trucking regulation. First, there are the direct costs of complying with trucking regulation, particularly the costs of applying for new licenses and opposing the applications of potential competitors. Bonsor (1980) estimated these to be $40 million annually for trucking firms alone. Second, there are the indirect costs imposed by licensing restrictions (e.g., the difficulties of reducing empty truck miles, increasing load factors, controlling mileage costs, and minimizing idle truck time). Third, the regulation of for-hire trucking led to the growth of private carriers partly because of the relatively high for-hire rates and partly because of the limited flexibility of for-hire carriers to respond to the needs of shippers. Fourth, trucking rates tend to be highest in those provinces with entry control and no effective rate regulation. Fifth, there is evidence that efficiency was lower and operating costs higher in Ontario and Quebec, two provinces that regulated trucking, than in Alberta.

Kim (1984) conducted an empirical study of the Canadian trucking industry to determine the beneficiaries of trucking regulation. Kim collected financial data on trucking firms from the 1975 Motor Carriers' Freight Survey and shipments data from the 1975 For-Hire Trucking Origin and Destination Survey. His econometric analysis revealed that "the existing regulatory structure, by inducing suboptimal levels of truck capacity utilization, benefits all factors of production and in particular benefits drivers, helpers, terminal workers, and fuel suppliers." Very large cost reductions can be obtained by reducing the amount of idle truck capacity. For example, a 10 percent increase in the level of capacity utilization is associated with a 9.9 percent savings in labour. (Savings are also apparent in fuel and materials.) Kim suggested that in the absence of trucking regulation, the level of capacity utilization would increase, with the result that the demand for all factors of production, but especially labour, would fall. "Technical inefficiency induced by excess input usage, as well as allocative inefficiency induced by the wrong proportion of input usage, will tend to diminish."

Both the Economic Council of Canada (1981) and Palmer (1991) were of the view that trucking regulation may have prevented firms from realizing the available scale economies (although the Council believed that these were unlikely to be substantial). While deregulation could lead to an increase in concentration in some trucking markets as firms strived to reach MES, the removal of entry restrictions should permit potential and actual competition to restrain the incumbent firms' abilities to exploit market power.

The costs of trucking regulation and the potential benefits of deregulation were recognized in the proposals for regulatory reform contained in the document *Freedom to Move*. The Minister of Transport proposed shifting the burden of proof on entry from the applicant to the party opposing entry, eliminating rate approval, creating a list of commodities and services exempt from control, streamlining operating licenses and license categories, and streamlining the license application process. The Minister also wanted to change the entry criterion from a test of "public convenience and necessity" to a "fit, willing and able" requirement.

Changes to trucking regulation were carried out in the *National Transportation Act, 1987* and the *Motor Vehicle Transport Act, 1987*.[22] The latter act required that the opponents of an application for a license to operate a trucking operation show that the operation of the extra-provincial trucking operation would likely be detrimental to the public interest. The act further stated that a provincial transport board may not attach any restrictions or conditions to a license for an extra-provincial truck undertaking.

Since the *National Transportation Act, 1987* and the *Motor Vehicle Transport Act, 1987* were enacted, there has been significant deregulation of trucking. This deregulation has been the result of federal-provincial agreements and new legislation. In 1989, Ontario's *Truck Transportation Act* was passed, and according to Madar (2000, p. 161) "By early

---

[22] Partial deregulation of the U.S. trucking industry was accomplished with the passage of the *Motor Carrier Act* in 1980. This Act reduced the barriers to entry into interstate trucking and removed the antitrust exemption from tariff bureaus. See Palmer (1991) for a brief discussion of trucking deregulation in the U.S.

1990 all major American carriers who had sought Ontario authorities now possessed them and began appearing quickly on Ontario's highways." Deregulation proceeded at different paces in different provinces. According to Madar, in 1992, Transport Canada reported to parliament that while Ontario and Quebec had moved to a fitness-only standard, in other provinces (such as New Brunswick), trucking was still substantially regulated.

Under the Agreement on Internal Trade between the federal and provincial governments, which came into effect in 1995, the provinces were to deregulate intra-provincial trucking, while the federal government agreed to repeal the section of the *Motor Vehicle Transport Act, 1987* that regulated intra-provincial operations by extra-provincial undertakings. The date of this repeal was postponed until 2000.

The effects of deregulation on the trucking industry have received little empirical attention. In one recent study, Woudsma and Kanaroglou (1996) examined the effects of the *Truck Transportation Act* in Ontario. The authors found that shipment rates declined for the truckload segment of the industry, and that there was not a significant increase in rates to less accessible regions. Further studies would be required to reach any strong conclusions regarding the effects of trucking deregulation in Canada.

Airline Regulation and Deregulation

In April 1937, Trans-Canada Airlines (TCA) was created by an act of Parliament on a common-stock basis, with the CNR as the sole shareholder. CP Air was formed by the amalgamation of ten local air carriers by the CPR in 1942. In 1944, the Air Transport Board was created under the *Aeronautics Act* and was responsible for regulating the airline industry.[23]

TCA was created to establish transcontinental air service and to provide service to both large and small communities. The Crown airline cross-subsidized certain routes and regions in order to ensure a uniform (distance related) fare structure across Canada. It could maintain cross subsidies because of entry and fare regulations that prevented competition from undermining them. From 1938 to 1959, TCA had a monopoly on every domestic route that it flew. Starting with CP Air's entry on the Vancouver-Montreal route in 1959, the federal government began to allow some entry onto routes. However,

---

[23] This summary of the history of the airline industry can be found in Christopher (1989).

price regulation was maintained on fares, and service regulation was used to prevent quality competition, particularly the frequency and scheduling of flights, from eroding profits.[24]

Besides TCA and CP Air, a number of regional carriers had grown and developed networks by the mid-1960s, but it was unclear where they fit into the regulated market. In 1966 and 1969, the Minister of Transport issued policy statements that set out regional air policy. According to Barone, Javidan, Reschenthaler, and Kraft (1986), Canada was divided into five regional markets served by different carriers who were restricted in the types of aircraft used and permitted to operate local and regional routes to supplement, not directly compete with, Air Canada (TCA's name had been changed to Air Canada in 1964) and CP Air. The five regions and the carriers serving them were as follows: B.C. and Alberta by Pacific Western Airlines (PWA); Saskatchewan, Manitoba and north-western Ontario by Transair; the remainder of Ontario and northwest Quebec by Nordair; all of Quebec east of Montreal by Quebecair; and the Atlantic provinces and Montreal by Eastern Provincial Airways. PWA acquired 73 percent of Transair in 1977, Air Canada acquired 86.5 percent of Nordair in 1978, the Province of Quebec acquired control of Quebecair in 1981, and CP Air acquired 100 percent of Eastern Provincial Airways in 1984. CP Air also acquired control of Nordair from Innocan (which had bought Air Canada's shares of Nordair in 1984) in 1986, eventually obtained control of Quebecair by 1987, and CP Air itself merged with PWA in 1987.[25]

Besides the national and regional carriers, there were also third level carriers that augmented the services of the regional carriers. These airlines included Time Air, Air Ontario, Air BC, and Norcanair. The third level carriers eventually ended up under the control of Air Canada and Pacific Western Airlines.

Christopher (1989) reports that in 1967, the government decided that CP Air would be allowed to increase its transcontinental services until it was providing 25 percent of the total transcontinental capacity by 1970. (CP Air eventually grew to about one-third of Air Canada's size.) Also in 1967, the Canadian Transport Commission (CTC) was created under the *National Transportation Act*, and it replaced the Air Transport Board as the airline industry's regulator.

---

[24] See Gillen, Oum, and Tretheway (1989).
[25] See Gillen, Stanbury, and Tretheway (1988).

The next major event to affect the airline industry in the 1970s (besides the expansion of Advanced Booking Charters and charter carriers like Wardair) was the passage of the *Air Canada Act* in November 1977. This Act placed Air Canada on the same regulatory footing as its competitors and encouraged Air Canada to "have due regard to sound business principles, and in particular the contemplation of profit" (see Economic Council of Canada, 1981, p. 29). Partly as a result of the changes taking place in the airline industry, in March of 1979, the government removed all capacity restrictions on CP Air and it was allowed to compete head-to-head with Air Canada.

In 1978, the *Airline Deregulation Act* was passed in the U.S. This Act took the pricing and route award decisions away from the Civil Aeronautics Board (which had regulated the U.S. airline industry since 1938) and allowed the airlines to make these decisions. (See Carlton and Perloff, 2004, Ch. 20, for a discussion of airline deregulation in the U.S.) The Board's regulation of the industry was to be phased out over a four-year period, with authority over routes to end on December 31, 1981, and authority over fares to end on January 1, 1983. During the transition period, a certain degree of fare setting flexibility was permitted and entry restrictions were eased.

Deregulation of the U.S. airline industry placed competitive pressure on Canadian airlines because of actual and potential diversion of international and transborder traffic to U.S. carriers. In 1978, Canadian airlines began to offer discount fares (subject to restrictions), and in 1979, Air Canada had its first "seat sale" offering heavily discounted fares. Still, pressure was mounting to deregulate the Canadian airline industry in order to achieve the same benefits (e.g., lower fares and variety of service offerings) as U.S. airline deregulation. The Economic Council of Canada (1981), in its report on *Reforming Regulation*, recommended opening the airline industry to new entry and also recommended that all carriers be allowed to cut fares, but not to increase them above the rate of inflation without the approval of the Canadian Transport Commission.

The Department of Transport released a set of policy proposals in August 1981 that would maintain CTC control of entry. In April 1982, the House of Commons Standing Committee on Transport released a report entitled *Domestic Air Carrier Policy*. While the report rejected the Department of Transport's proposals, it recommended that regulation of the airline industry continue, but with greater competition permitted over time.[26]

---

[26] See Reschenthaler and Stanbury (1983) for a more detailed discussion of the Department of Transport's and House of Commons Standing Committee on Transport's proposals.

In May of 1984, the Minister of Transport, Lloyd Axworthy, announced a policy which relaxed airline regulation somewhat. Christopher (1989) notes that geographic restrictions on carriers were lifted, license restrictions were removed, and greater price flexibility was allowed. With the change from a Liberal to Conservative government in the fall of 1984 came the new government's proposals for further deregulation of the airline industry. These were set out in the document *Freedom to Move* in July 1985, and included the following:

(1) entry to any class of domestic commercial air service will be governed by a "fit, willing and able" requirement, instead of the "public convenience and necessity" test. Compliance with safety regulations and proof of insurance were deemed to meet this requirement;
(2) market exit will not be impeded except by a requirement of advance notice;
(3) there will be no ongoing regulation of domestic fares, but the National Transportation Agency would be able to review fare increases on appeal, and overturn them if they were found excessive.

These proposals were largely carried out with the passage of the *National Transportation Act* in 1987. In addition, the Act permitted the Minister of Transport to provide financial assistance in order to maintain air services deemed essential, the Act protected essential services to northern and remote areas, and it gave the National Transportation Agency the power to review and reject unreasonable fare increases. International air service was still to be determined through bilateral air agreements between Canada and other countries. The *National Transportation Act* was replaced in 1996 by the *Canada Transportation Act*.

Economists largely favoured deregulation of the airline industry because they believed that actual and potential entry and competition would force airlines to be efficient and to maintain competitive fares. While there was little evidence to support the proposition that airlines operated in perfectly contestable markets, there was evidence from the U.S. experience with deregulation that airlines were becoming more efficient and airline fares were moving closer to costs (see Bailey, Graham, and Kaplan, 1985). There was also increasing evidence, however, that entry barriers in the airline industry might be higher than anticipated prior to deregulation, and this was of particular concern in the Canadian context given developments in the Canadian airline industry.

In 1987, PWA and Canadian Pacific Air Lines merged to form Canadian Airlines International Ltd. (CAIL), a subsidiary of PWA Corp. Also in 1987, Air Canada and CAIL merged their respective reservation systems to form Gemini.[27] In 1989, CAIL acquired Wardair, originally a charter carrier that made an unsuccessful attempt to compete with Air Canada and Canadian in scheduled air service. By 1990, Air Canada and Canadian had acquired or formed alliances with virtually all of the local service and regional air carriers. Also of significance was the privatization of Air Canada, which occurred via two share offerings in 1988 and 1989.

In 1999, Canadian Airlines was acquired by Air Canada. During the 1990s, several small carriers entered Canadian markets, with limited success. WestJet, which was founded in 1996 and initially focused on western Canadian routes, had expanded its network to 24 cities across the country by 2004. Other small air carriers offering scheduled passenger service in Canada, including CanJetI and Royal, have been unsuccessful. Two recent entrants into the Canadian airline industry, CanJetII and Jetsgo, are still operating at the time of writing.

As of 2002, the Canadian scheduled air travel industry was largely dominated by Air Canada. According to Statistics Canada (2002), Air Canada accounted for 64 percent of passengers carried by Canadian air carriers and 86 percent of passenger-kilometres in 2002. (Foreign carriers also serve transborder and international routes.)

Despite its dominance among Canadian carriers, in April 2003 Air Canada obtained an order from the Ontario Superior Court of Justice providing creditor protection under the *Companies' Creditors Arrangements Act.* While it might be tempting to blame deregulation of the airline industry for the financial problems confronting certain Canadian air carriers and for the presence of a dominant airline, such a conclusion should not be drawn without evidence obtained from careful studies of the operation of the Canadian airline industry since deregulation.

In the 1990s, a limited degree of liberation of international air service was obtained through the 1995 Open Skies agreement between Canada and the U.S. Under this agreement Canadian airlines could provide unrestricted service from any Canadian city

---

[27] Gillen, Stanbury, and Tretheway (1988) discuss the history and consequences of the structural changes that occurred in Canada's airline industry through 1987.

to any U.S. city, while U.S. airlines could provide unrestricted service from any U.S. city to any Canadian city except Montreal, Toronto and Vancouver, where liberalization was phased in over two to three years. Recently, the *Canada Transportation Act* Review Panel recommended that the government should negotiate an agreement with the U.S. and Mexico to allow North American carriers to compete freely throughout the continent.[28] However, Lazar (2003, p. 2) argues that "even if the Government of Canada did succeed in negotiating more open, bilateral or multilateral agreements, there is no assurance that there would be any significant impact on the degree of competition in the Canadian market."

IV. OTHER REGULATED INDUSTRIES

There are other major industries subject to economic regulation in Canada. Space permits only a brief description of those regulations here.

In most provinces, investor-owned utilities supplying electricity and natural gas are subject to regulation by provincial public utility boards. Where Crown corporations supply electricity and/or natural gas, the provincial public utility boards may still exercise some degree of regulation.

The National Energy Board (NEB) regulates the interprovincial transmission of natural gas and oil. Companies such as TransCanada Pipelines and Interprovincial Pipeline would be subject to the NEB's regulation of tolls. The prices of oil and natural gas were deregulated in 1985 and 1986, respectively. Controls on oil exports were also largely eliminated in 1985.[29]

Regulation in Canadian agriculture is largely accomplished through agricultural marketing boards. Marketing boards are compulsory marketing agents that perform certain marketing functions on behalf of producers. According to Veeman (1997), marketing boards operate under federal authority, provincial authority, or under the joint authority of both federal and provincial governments. Veeman (1997) reports that as of 1997 there were over 100 provincial marketing boards, in addition to national marketing boards. Commodities subject to marketing boards include grains, dairy products, hogs, poultry, eggs, and fruit.

---

[28] See Government of Canada (2001).

[29] For a detailed discussion of deregulation of the oil and gas industries, see Watkins (1991).

Historically, the Economic Council of Canada (1981) has divided marketing boards into two categories: commodity boards and supervisory boards. There are five groups of commodity boards, distinguished by the powers delegated to them. These boards are described as (1) promotional boards, (2) negotiating boards, (3) central selling boards, (4) boards that regulate prices and output, and (5) supply management boards. The supervisory boards include those with supervisory responsibility over individual commodity boards.

As of May 2004, several provinces were regulating the retail prices of gasoline. In PEI, the Island Regulatory and Appeals Commission sets minimum and maximum prices for each company. In Newfoundland, the Petroleum Products Pricing Commission sets region-specific maximum prices. Price floors are used in Quebec to limit price wars, which were taken by independent retailers to be signs of predation.[30] Finally, in May 2004, the government of Nova Scotia tabled the *Petroleum Product Pricing Act,* which would require wholesalers and the retailers owned or controlled by them to provide 48-hour notice of all price increases through a government website.

There are other types of regulation, such as occupational health and safety regulation and environmental regulation, that have significant impacts on the ways in which a firm conducts its business. Like other forms of regulation, these have been undergoing changes in recent years, and will likely be subject to additional changes in the future.

V. SUMMARY

This chapter has examined some of the most studied cases of regulation in Canada: the regulation of telecommunications and transportation industries.

Until quite recently, telephone companies acted as regional monopolies in the provision of local and long distance services. Those telephone companies subject to federal jurisdiction have been regulated by the CRTC, while those that are provincial Crown corporations have been regulated by the provincial government or provincial public utility boards. Since 1979, there has been a progressive relaxation of restrictions on competition in the telecommunications industry in Canada. Most recently, the CRTC

---

[30] See Gagne et al. (2003) for a discussion of the Quebec regulations and their motivations.

decision to permit the provision of competitive long-distance services, and the passage of the *Telecommunications Act,* have resulted in an increase in competition in the telecommunications industry. To date, this increase has been observed largely in long distance service, and it is unclear the extent to which deregulation will increase competition in local service.

Until the 1980s, transportation industries were subject to quite stringent regulations affecting entry, exit and pricing in their industries. Railway regulations affected the ability of railways to be competitive with trucks and distorted resource allocation within the railway industry. Trucking regulation made it difficult for the for-hire segment of the industry to compete with private trucking. Airline regulation reduced incentives for airlines to operate efficiently and made it difficult for Canadian airlines to compete with deregulated U.S. airlines. Recognition of these problems led the government to pass the *National Transportation Act* in 1987 and its successor, the *Canada Transportation Act.* Entry restrictions have been relaxed, the abandonment of uneconomic services has been made easier, and pricing flexibility has been greatly increased. Studies are needed to evaluate the effects of deregulation in transportation industries.

Finally, it was noted that other major industries in Canada, such as the public utility, oil and gas, agricultural industries, and gasoline retailing, have been and still are subject to a variety of regulations. Occupational health and safety regulation and environmental regulation also have significant impacts on the ways in which firms conduct their business in Canada.

Chapter 5

REFERENCES

Bailey, Elizabeth E., David R. Graham, and Daniel P. Kaplan. 1985. *Deregulating the Airlines*. Cambridge, Mass.: MIT Press.

Barone, S.S., Mansour Javidan, G.B. Reschenthaler, and Dennis J.H. Kraft. 1986. "Deregulation in the Canadian Airline Industry: Is There Room for a Large Regional Airline?" *Logistics and Transportation Review* 22: 421–448.

Blakney, John F. 1991. "Marathon CRTC Long Distance Competition Hearing Concludes," *Canadian Competition Policy Record* 12: 16–18.

Blakney, John F. 1992a. "CRTC Authorizes Increased Long Distance Competition," *Canadian Competition Policy Record* 13: 52–59.

Blakney, John F. 1992b. "Federal Court Denies Telephone Company Appeal of CRTC Long Distance Competition Decision," *Canadian Competition Policy Record* 13: 26–27.

Bonsor, Norman C. 1980. "The Impact of Regulation on For-Hire Highway Carriers: An Analysis of the Cost Borne by Carriers in the Production of Regulatory Decisions," in *Studies of Trucking Regulation: Vol. II*, Economic Council of Canada Regulation Reference Working Paper No. 3.

Bonsor, Norman C. 1984. *Transportation Economics: Theory and Canadian Policy*. Toronto: Butterworths.

Brock, G.W. 1981. *The Telecommunications Industry: The Dynamics of Market Structure*. Cambridge, Mass.: Harvard University Press.

Carlton, Dennis W. and Jeffrey M. Perloff. 2004. *Modern Industrial Organization*, Fourth Edition. New York: Pearson Education.

Christopher, John. 1989. "Airline Deregulation in Canada," Current Issue Review 89-2E, Research Branch, Library of Parliament.

CRTC. 2003. *Report to the Governor in Council: Status of Competition in Canadian Telecommunications Markets*. Ottawa: CRTC.

Economic Council of Canada. 1981. *Reforming Regulation*. Ottawa: Minister of Supply and Services Canada. Reproduced with the permission of the Minister of Public Works and Government Services, 2004.

Fuss, Melvyn and Leonard Waverman. 1981. "The Regulation of Telecommunications in Canada," Economic Council of Canada Regulation Reference Technical Report No. 7.

Gagne, Robert, Simon van Norden, and Bruno Versaevel. 2003. "Testing Optimal Punishment Mechanisms under Price Regulation: the Case of the Retail Market for Gasoline," CIRANO Scientific Series Working Paper 2003s-57.

164

Gillen, David W., Tae H. Oum, and Michael W. Tretheway. 1989. "Privatization of Air Canada: Why It Is Necessary in a Deregulated Environment," *Canadian Public Policy* 15: 285–299.

Gillen, David W., W.T. Stanbury, and Michael W. Tretheway. 1988. "Duopoly in Canada's Airline Industry: Consequences and Policy Issues," *Canadian Public Policy* 14: 15–31.

Globerman, Steven. 1986. "Economic Factors in Telecommunications Policy and Regulation," in W.T. Stanbury, ed., *Telecommunications Policy and Regulation: The Impact of Competition and Technological Change*. Montreal: Institute for Research on Public Policy.

Globerman, Steven. 1988. *Telecommunications in Canada*. Vancouver: The Fraser Institute.

Government of Canada. 2001. *Vision and Balance: Report of the Canada Transportation Act Review Panel*, Ottawa: Minister of Public Works and Government Services Canada.

Industry Canada. 2003. *Telecommunications Service in Canada: An Industry Overview*. Ottawa: Industry Canada. Updated versions of this material is available at http://strategis.ic.gc.ca/TelecomServicesOverview.

Kim, Moshe. 1984. "The Beneficiaries of Trucking Regulation, Revisited," *Journal of Law and Economics* 27: 227–241.

Lazar, Fred. 2003. "Turbulence in the Skies: Options for Making Canadian Airline Travel More Attractive," *C.D. Howe Institute Commentary* No. 181.

Loyns, R.M.A., Colin A. Carter, and Eric Peters. 1991. "Regulatory Change in Canadian Agriculture," in Walter Block and George Lermer, eds., *Breaking the Shackles: Deregulating Canadian Industry*. Vancouver: Fraser Institute.

Madar, Daniel. 2000. *Heavy Traffic: Deregulation, Trade, and Transformation in North American Trucking*. Vancouver: UBC Press.

Monteiro, Joseph. 2001. "Regulatory Reforms in Canadian Transportation Since 1987," *Proceedings of the 36th Annual Conference of the Canadian Transportation Research Forum*, 101–120.

National Transportation Agency of Canada. 1992. *Annual Report 1992*.

Norrie, Kenneth. 1983. "Not Much to Crow About: A Primer on the Statutory Grain Freight Rate Issue," *Canadian Public Policy* 9: 434–445.

Palmer, John P. 1988. *An Economic Analysis of Canada's Ground Transportation Sector*. Vancouver: Fraser Institute.

Palmer, John P. 1991. "Truck and Rail Shipping: The Deregulation Evolution," in

Walter Block and George Lermer, eds., *Breaking the Shackles: Deregulating Canadian Industry*. Vancouver: Fraser Institute.

Reschenthaler, G.B. and W.T. Stanbury. 1983. "Deregulating Canada's Airlines: Grounded by False Assumptions," *Canadian Public Policy* 9: 210–222.

Stanbury, W.T. and Fred Thompson. 1982. *Regulatory Reform in Canada*. Montreal: Institute for Research on Public Policy.

Stanbury, W.T. 1986. "Decision Making in Telecommunications: The Interplay of Distributional and Efficiency Considerations," in W.T. Stanbury, ed., *Telecommunications Policy and Regulation: The Impact of Competition and Technological Change*. Montreal: Institute for Research on Public Policy.

Stanbury, W.T. 1996a. "Competition Policy and the Regulation of Telecommunications in Canada," in W.T. Stanbury, ed., *Perspectives on the New Economics and Regulation of Telecommunications*. Montreal: The Institute for Research on Public Policy.

Stanbury, W.T. 1996b. "Chronology of Canadian Telecommunications: January 1992 to January 1996," in W.T. Stanbury, ed., *Perspectives on the New Economics and Regulation of Telecommunication*s. Montreal: The Institute for Research on Public Policy.

Statistics Canada. 2004. *Aviation Statistics Centre-Service Bulletin*. Catalogue 51-004-XIB, Vol. 36, No. 2.

Strick, John C. 1990. *The Economics of Government Regulation: Theory and Canadian Practice*. Toronto: Thompson Educational Publishing Inc.

Veeman, Michele M. 1997. "Marketing Boards: The Canadian Experience Revisited," *Canadian Journal of Agricultural Economics* 45: 411–420.

Watkins, G. Campbell. 1991. "Deregulation and the Canadian Petroleum Industry: Adolescence or Maturity?" in Walter Block and George Lermer, eds., *Breaking the Shackles: Deregulating Canadian Industry*. Vancouver: Fraser Institute.

Woudsma, Clarence G. and Pavlos S. Kanaroglou. 1996. "The Impacts of Trucking Deregulation in Ontario: A Market Specific Analysis," Canadian Public Policy 22: 356–377.